17.

STANDARD GRADE HISTORY

International Relations 1890–1930

Second edition

JA Harkness, H McMillan and D Moore

Hodder & Stoughton

A MEMBER OF THE HODDER HEADLINE GROUP

ACKNOWLEDGEMENTS

The Publishers would like to thank the following for permission to reproduce material in this volume:

Basil Blackwell for the extract from *The First World War* by Barry Bates; Blackie And Son Ltd for the extracts from *The First World War* by L F Hobley (1971); Malcolm Brown for the extracts from *Christmas Truce* by Brown and Seaton (1984); Collins/Angus & Robertson for the extract from *Behind the Lines: One Woman's War* by A J P Taylor (1961); Heinemann Ltd for the extracts from *Daily Mail* dated April 2nd 1915; Faber and Faber Ltd for the extracts from *Old Soldiers Never Die* by Frank Richards; Hamish Hamilton for the extract from *The Origins of the Second World War* by A J P Taylor (1961); Heinemann Ltd for the extracts from *War Beyond Britain* by Fiona Reynoldson and *The Drift to War* by Stone; HMSO for the extracts from *Documents on the origins of the war 1898–1914* by G P Gooch and H W Temperley (1930); Michael Joseph Ltd for the extracts from *Voices and Images of the Great War* by Lyn Macdonald © Lyn Macdonald 1988; Longman Group Ltd for the extracts from *Europe 1880–1945* by J M Roberts (1967), *The League and the U.N.O.* by Gibbons and Morican, and *The Weimar Republic* by J W Hiden (1984); Macmillan Publishers Ltd for the extract from *Useful Toil* ed. J Burnett; Macmillan Publishing Company (USA) for the extracts from *The Genesis of War* by H H Asquith (Cassell, 1923), *Memoirs and Reflections, Volume 2* by H H Asquith (Cassell, 1928) and *The German High Seas* by Admiral Reinhard Scheer (Cassell, 1920); Methuen & Co. for the extracts from *Britain Between the Wars* by C L Mowat; Mirror Group Newspapers Ltd for the extracts from *The Daily Record* dated May 8th 1917; extracts from *Speeches and Documents in American History* by Robert Birley (1942) and *Twentieth Century Britain* (2nd Edition) by W Robson (1983) reproduced by permission of Oxford University Press; extracts from *White Heat* by John Terraine reprinted by permission of the Peters Fraser & Dunlop Group Ltd; *'In Flanders fields'* by John McCrae, reproduced by permission of Punch (1915); *'Suicide in the Trenches'* by Siegfried Sassoon reproduced by permission of George Sassoon; Secker and Warburg for the extract from *The Twelve Days* by George Malcolm Thomson (1964); Sheil Land Associates Ltd for the extracts from *Voices 1870–1914* © Peter Vansittart; the extract from *Turn of the century* by Hoare reproduced by permission of Simon & Schuster Young Books, Hemel Hempstead, UK; Thames & Hudson Ltd for the extracts from *From Sarajevo to Potsdam* by A J P Taylor; Stanley Thornes for the extract from *Europe in Conflict – A History of Europe 1870–1970* by A Jamieson; the Trustees of the Imperial War Museum for the extracts from *With a Machine Gun to Cambrai* by G Coppard; A P Watt Ltd, on behalf of the Trustees of the Robert Graves Copyright Trust for the extracts from *Goodbye To All That* by R Graves (1929).

Every effort has been made to trace and acknowledge ownership of copyright. The publishers will be glad to make suitable arrangements with any copyright holders whom it has not been possible to contact.

The publishers would like to thank the following for permission to reproduce copyright illustrations:

Author p 1; Bild Archiv der Osterreichischen Nationalbibliothik, Wien p 31 both; David Low–Evening Standard/Centre for the Study of Cartoons and Caricature, University of Kent at Canterbury/Solo Syndication p 91 right; Edimedia p 8, 26 left; Illustrated London News Picture Library p 32 right; Imperial War Museum cover, p 17, 21, 28 right, 37, 41 both, 42, 47, 54, 68 left both, 75, 76, 78 right; Mansell Collection p 22, 26 right; 27 bottom right and top, 28 left, 30, 34, 36 left; Popperfoto p 3, 11, 18; Reproduced by permission of Punch p 2, 5, 6 right, 14 both, 19, 32 left, 36 right, 39, 43, 71, 86, 87, 88; The Hulton Picture Company p 6 top, 7, 33, 40, 49, 77; Ullstein Bilderdienst p 44, 45; Weimar Archive p 27 bottom left.

Orders: please contact Bookpoint Ltd, 39 Milton Park, Abingdon, Oxon OX14 4TD. Telephone: (44) 01235 400414, Fax: (44) 01235 400454. Lines are open from 9.00–6.00, Monday to Saturday, with a 24 hour message answering service. Email address: orders@bookpoint.co.uk

A catalogue record for this title is available from The British Library

ISBN 0 340 74318 2

Published by Hodder & Stoughton Educational Scotland
First published 1999
Impression number 10 9 8 7 6 5 4 3 2 1
Year 2004 2003 2002 2001 2000 1999

Copyright © 1999 James Harkness, Hugh McMillan and David Moore

All rights reserved. No part of this publication may be reproduced or transmitted in any form or by any means, electronic or mechanical, including photocopy, recording, or any information storage and retrieval system, without permission in writing from the publisher or under licence from the Copyright Licensing Agency Limited. Further details of such licences (for reprographic reproduction) may be obtained from the Copyright Licensing Agency Limited, of 90 Tottenham Court Road, London W1P 9HE.

Cover photograph from The Imperial War Museum

Illustrations by Richard Duszczak and David Hancock.

Typeset by Fakenham Photosetting Ltd, Fakenham, Norfolk
Printed in Great Britain for Hodder & Stoughton Educational, a division of Hodder Headline Plc, 338 Euston Road, London NW1 3BH by Redwood Books Ltd, Trowbridge, Wiltshire.

Contents

PREFACE

This text in the STANDARD GRADE HISTORY series has been revised to take account of changes in the examinable content and criteria of the Standard Grade examination, including those which will come into effect in 1999. Each book is a blend of narrative and source evidence, both written and visual. Chapters consist of two parts, the first designed for pupils working towards success at Foundation/General level and the second supporting those aiming at General/Credit level. Activities are suggested which support the overall aims of the course, the different sections of each chapter **and** the demands of the external examination. The questions in the Activities sections have been coded according to whether they involve Knowledge and Understanding (KU), Enquiry Skills (ENQ) or Investigation (INV).

Graeme Coy, 1999

1 We are the Dead

F/G/C

Co-operation and Conflict

Source 1.1 The grave of Private Donald Snaddon of the Royal Scots Fusiliers who died on 18 January 1916 at Ypres, aged 15.

Among the graves in another cemetery near Ypres, an army surgeon called John McCrae noticed poppies growing and he wrote these words:

Source 1.2

In Flanders fields the poppies blow.
Between the crosses, row on row
That mark our place; and in the sky
The larks still bravely singing, fly,
Scarce heard amid the groans below.
We are the Dead. Short days ago
We lived, felt dawn, saw sunset glow,
Loved and were loved, and now we lie
In Flanders fields.

Written by John McCrae during the 2nd Battle of Ypres, 1915

In 1900 Donald Snaddon was born in Glasgow. During the period he lived in Partick, Europe was united in a way which has not been matched since (according to the historian AJP Taylor).

Source 1.3

In 1914 Europe was a single civilized community. A man could travel across the whole continent without a passport until he reached Russia or the Turkish Empire.

AJP Taylor, 'From Sarajevo to Potsdam'.

When Snaddon was at his first lessons he might have heard about the German Emperor, Kaiser Wilhelm II. Germany already had a large army and from 1900 onwards, Wilhelm began to build a large navy. Germany's European neighbours were worried by the Kaiser's actions and formed alliances to protect themselves from Germany.

In August 1914 Britain went to war and Donald Snaddon broke the law and joined the army. He trained as a soldier and by January 1916 he lay dead in a field in Flanders (Belgium) – a victim of the Great War.

For four long years the war dragged on. When it finished in November 1918, the casualty lists were truly horrific.

Source 1.4 Numbers killed during the First World War.

Great Britain	761 213
France	1 385 000
Russia	1 700 000 (estimate)
Germany	2 000 000
Austria-Hungary	1 100 000

F/G/C THE HISTORICAL JIGSAW

International Relations 1890–1930

Studying this period in history is like doing a jigsaw. Before we can see the whole picture all the pieces have to be fitted together. The 'pieces' in history are called evidence and in writing this book we have used evidence to describe events, to explain why certain things happened, and to explain why people acted as they did. Through the words and images of the people who lived at the time we hope to bring the story to life.

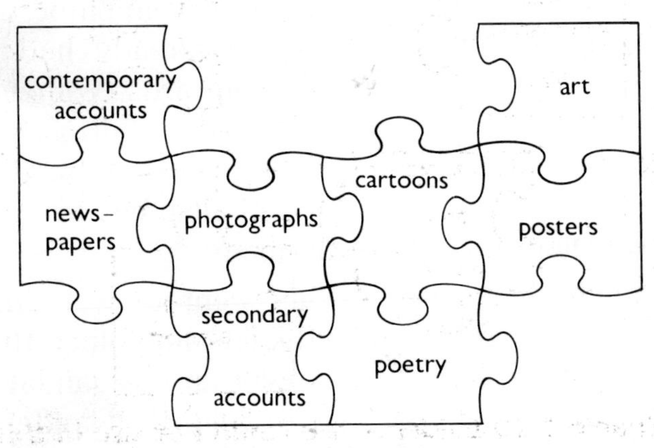

Source 1.5 The Jigsaw of Evidence.

In a book, it is only possible to choose a few examples from these sources of information, and we have only been able to choose sources which can be printed.

Example 1 – Cartoons

In the nineteenth and early twentieth centuries, a magazine called *Punch* was widely read. This satirical magazine commented on current affairs and contained many cartoons which commented on the major political issues of the day. As well as magazines like *Punch*, most people read newspapers. With no radio or TV at that time this was the only way to keep up with what was happening in the world, and extracts from contemporary newspapers have also been used. Newspapers also used cartoons to comment on events and we have used examples of these throughout the book as well.

[Reproduced by permission of the Proprietors of 'Punch.'

L'ENFANT TERRIBLE!

CHORUS IN THE STERN. "DON'T GO ON LIKE THAT—OR YOU'LL UPSET US ALL!"

Source 1.6 This British cartoon shows how the Kaiser was causing instability in Europe before 1914.

Cartoons like this are useful because they show complicated actions in a simple way. However, historians must beware of bias in sources like this.

Example 2 – Poetry

Source 1.7 Suicide in the Trenches

I knew a simple soldier boy
Who grinned at life in empty joy,
Slept soundly through the lonesome dark,
and whistled early with the lark.

In winter trenches, cowed and glum,
With crumps and lice and lack of rum,
He put a bullet through his brain.
No-one spoke of him again.

You smug-faced crowds with kindling eye
Who cheer when soldier lads march by,
Sneak home and pray you'll never know
The hell where youth and laughter go.

Siegfried Sassoon, 1917.

From war poetry we can learn about the experience of war and also about the attitudes of some of those who fought.

Example 3 – Photographs

Source 1.8 Trench conditions.

In 1914–1918 war was horrific and some cameramen went to war and took pictures of the horrors. These photographs now give us a first class record of events from the war. We have made great use of photographs in the book. As you look at them, work out which of them might have been used for propaganda.

Example 4 – Contemporary accounts

This account of an incident in the trenches was written by Frank Richards in a book called *Old Soldiers Never Die.*

Source 1.9

We took turns in one part of the trench bailing out water with a bucket. One morning, a man named Davies had his thumb shot off whilst bailing. The next man deliberately invited a bullet through his hands by exposing them a little longer than necessary – but the bucket got riddled instead.

There are many examples of soldiers who wrote about their experiences. These accounts are valuable to us since the soldiers describe the events in which they took part.

Missing evidence

Listed above are only a few examples of the kinds of evidence we have been able to use to build up a picture of the events of the years between 1890 and 1930. We could not use all the evidence in a book. Instead, you should try to make use of some of the following types of source in your study of this period. In that way you will learn a lot more and the experience will be more enjoyable.

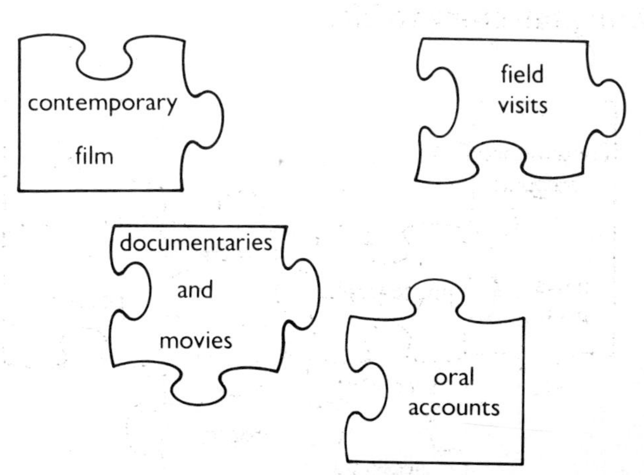

Source 1.10 Evidence we could not use in this book.

The period 1890–1930 was full of excitement and drama. In these years the old world of the nineteenth century disappeared for ever and a new era began. America became a major power, Britain's importance declined and the horrors of war led people to try to settle future quarrels in other ways. Through the words and images of those who lived in the time, this book tries to capture the excitement of the period.

Activities

1. Explain why using evidence is so important in History. (ENQ)
2. In what ways are contemporary sources like Sources 1.6, 1.7, 1.8 and 1.9 useful for historians? (ENQ)
3. **Class Discussion**: What features of a source are important in deciding whether or not it is valuable to a historian. (ENQ)

2 THE KAISER'S GERMANY

F/G

[Reproduced by permission of the Proprietors of 'Punch.'

DROPPING THE PILOT.

Punch's most famous political cartoon. William II and Bismarck part company. Both of them, strangely enough, liked this representation.

Source 2.1 Bismarck steps down from the ship Germany leaving Kaiser Wilhelm in sole charge – a Punch cartoon from 1890.

In 1890 there was a change in the leadership of Germany. Bismarck, who had been Chancellor for many years, was dropped from the government. For 20 years he had kept Germany at peace. He was always careful in dealing with other world leaders and encouraged them not to fear Germany. Bismarck had controlled German affairs and even told the Kaiser what to do! But, in 1888, Wilhelm II became Kaiser and he was not willing to listen to Bismarck.

Source 2.2

> ***There is only one master in Germany and I am he.***
>
> **Kaiser Wilhelm II, 1888.**

Kaiser Wilhelm was not like Bismarck. He was rude, impulsive and always wanted things done his way. He also had such a terrible temper that even members of the German government thought he might be mad.

Kaiser Wilhelm's strange behaviour meant that he was not trusted by politicians. But then the Kaiser did not trust them either. 'My trust,' he said, 'is placed in the army'. When the military offered advice, the Kaiser listened. The advice they gave alarmed those who wanted peace, for the Kaiser was reminded that wars had brought Germany glory, wealth and territory. The Kaiser claimed that building up the army showed his peaceful intentions. He said:

Source 2.3

> ***He who wishes for peace, let him prepare for war.***
>
> **Kaiser Wilhelm II, 1890.**

Source 2.4 The Kaiser in uniform – this was his favourite form of dress.

Source 2.5 This table shows the number of soldiers the Great Powers had.

	1880	1914
Germany	1 300 000	5 000 000
France	740 000	4 000 000
Russia	400 000	1 200 000
Austria–Hungary	770 000	800 000
Britain	400 000	700 000

Germany was the strongest country in Europe. Kaiser Wilhelm II, who came to power in 1890 however, was not satisfied with what Germany had. He admired the British Empire and wanted colonies for Germany. 'Germany must have its place in the sun', he announced. However, Germany had entered the race for colonies too late as the world was now divided up amongst the other Great Powers. 'How would Germany obtain colonies?' people asked. 'The world belongs to the strong', came the reply.

The Kaiser's huge army meant that any threat he made was taken seriously. Some Germans thought that the other Great Powers took the Kaiser too seriously.

Source 2.6

He only wanted to impress them so that they'd think that he was another Napoleon or Frederick the Great.

Prince von Bülow, German Chancellor 1900–1909.

The Kaiser believed Germany to be so strong that she need fear no one, but he was a vain and very proud man. He ignored the advice of experienced statesmen, like Otto von Bismarck, that Germany must prevent countries forming alliances against her, especially France, Britain and Russia.

Source 2.7

These three would make an Alliance against Germany more dangerous than any other she might face.

Otto von Bismarck, 1885.

However, France, Britain and Russia disliked each other so much that, in 1890, such an alliance was impossible. Even so, a growing fear of Germany very soon placed them all in the same boat.

[Reproduced by permission of the Proprietors of 'Punch.'

L'ENFANT TERRIBLE!

CHORUS IN THE STERN. "DON'T GO ON LIKE THAT—OR YOU'LL UPSET US ALL!"

Source 2.8 The cartoon shows that the Kaiser's antics alarmed other European leaders.

Activities

1. What do Sources 2.1 and 2.2 tell us about the power of the Kaiser? (KU)
2. To what extent do Sources 2.1 and 2.2 agree that Kaiser Wilhelm II was in complete control of Germany? (ENQ)
3. According to Sources 2.3, 2.4 and 2.5, why might a rival country fear Germany more after 1890? (KU)
4. (a) What alliance of countries did Bismarck fear most?
   (b) Why was such an alliance unlikely in 1890? (KU)
5. **Discussion:** Work in pairs using Sources 2.2, 2.3, 2.5, 2.6 and the text to help you.
   The Kaiser said, 'I want . . .'
   a) Write down three possible endings to this sentence.
   b) Write down an explanation for each completed statement.
   Discuss your answers. (KU)

C QUARRELSOME NEIGHBOURS

France quarrels with Germany

France was the only great power which seemed determined on war with Germany. French hostility was due to the events of 1871. In that year, France – the most powerful nation in the world – was defeated and humiliated by Germany.

Source 2.9

> ***I can feel already the coming of that immense revenge . . . Oh! then France will be a power to reckon with. We will see her at a single stroke, resume possession of Alsace–Lorraine.***
>
> **Victor Hugo speaking to the French parliament, 1872.**

Defeat cost the French people more than hurt pride. France was forced to pay Germany huge sums in reparations and give up the valuable border lands of Alsace–Lorraine.

Source 2.10 The birth of the German Empire is announced from the Hall of Mirrors, Versailles.

A successful war of revenge may have seemed attractive to many French people but by 1890 there seemed little chance of the dream becoming reality. In 1870, their ill-equipped and badly led soldiers had been easily beaten by the German army. In Germany every able-bodied man was liable for military service. He would be called up, trained and then returned to civilian life to be in reserve should war break out. However, this was something the French could copy and soon two years training was compulsory for every 20 year old man. In 1913 this was increased to three years as tension between Germany and France increased.

Source 2.11 French children stand beside an 1871 war memorial and gaze over the lost lands of Alsace–Lorraine.

However training alone could not make France a match for Germany. The population of Germany was increasing at a faster rate than that of France. In 1890 both countries had around 40 million people but while by 1910 the population of France had barely grown, that of Germany had risen to over 58 million. This meant that Germany would always have more soldiers than France. However an army can do little without weapons, but here too Germany had a growing advantage. In the later years of the nineteenth century, the industrial development of Germany was breathtaking, especially in those industries associated with war as shown in Source 2.12.

Source 2.12 Steel produced each year in millions of tons.

	1890	1900	1910
Britain	3.6	5.0	6.5
France	0.7	1.6	3.4
Germany	2.2	6.6	13.7
Russia	0.4	2.2	3.5
Italy	0.1	0.1	0.7

From JM Roberts, Europe 1880–1945, 1967.

Clearly, France needed an ally but in 1890, she had more enemies than friends.

Britain and France: Imperial rivals

During the nineteenth century, Britain proudly assembled the world's largest Empire from which she could gather raw materials for her factories, food for her people and soldiers for her army. However, as the number of Great Powers involved in Empire building increased, so too did the risk of war. The 'Scramble for Africa', especially, caused a great deal of ill feeling particularly between France and Britain. These two became such bitter rivals over colonies that war between them seemed likely, for example in 1898 when a crisis erupted over the small town of Fashoda in Sudan. When Britain claimed ownership, France was outraged to such an extent that even Alsace–Lorraine became, for the moment, of secondary importance.

Source 2.13

> ***Our hatred of Germany can be wiped out but England is the enemy of yesterday, tomorrow and forever.***

French journalist, 1898.

Britain and France: Enemies of Russia

Britain and Russia were not on good terms in 1890. Russian ambition in the Balkans was seen as a threat to Britain's trade route through the Suez Canal. Furthermore, it was believed that Russia wanted to rule India, one of the most valuable parts of the British Empire.

Like Britain, France was by tradition an enemy of Russia. The two countries had very different systems of government, with the leader of France elected by the people while the leader of Russia was believed to be chosen by God. Bismarck's fear that France, Britain and Russia might unite against Germany therefore seemed very unlikely at that time.

Britain quarrels with Germany

In 1899 Britain went to war with two tiny South African Boer Republics. It took the British army three years to defeat an army of farmers. British tactics (such as the widespread use of concentration camps for prisoners) were widely condemned, both in Britain and in other countries.

The Kaiser openly supported the Boers and twice suggested an alliance of the other Great Powers against Britain. However, such an alliance was not formed, mainly because of the strength of the Royal Navy. The Boer War was therefore of great importance for several reasons. Firstly, Britain used to regard its isolation as 'splendid' but now the absence of allies was seen as a disadvantage. Secondly, the importance of a strong navy was more greatly appreciated in Britain and in Germany. The Kaiser now saw an even greater need for a high seas fleet of his own. Thirdly, those British politicians who had since 1898 been proposing an alliance between Britain and Germany – fell silent. The Kaiser's actions during the Boer War ensured that Germany was seen more as a threat, than as a friend. But would fear of Germany become strong enough to force Britain, France and Russia to forget their differences?

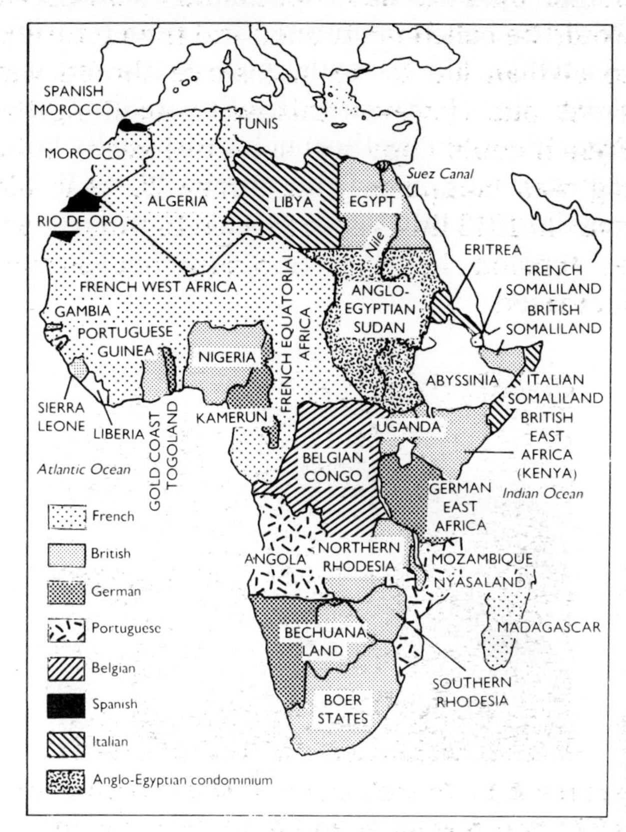

Source 2.14 By the time Germany entered the scramble for Africa the most valuable areas had been seized.

Britain enters the arms race

A dismal performance in the Boer War and the developing arms race in Europe forced Britain to look at ways of improving the British army. In 1904 the General Staff was created to improve overall planning and tactics. British policy on recruitment was also reviewed but despite the growth of mass armies in Europe and the widespread use of conscription, Lord Haldane (Minister for War) decided to have only a small army and to enlist only volunteers. His response to growing international tension was to create the British Expeditionary Force – an army of 160 000 well-equipped, professional soldiers which would be ready for immediate travel to trouble spots in Europe or the Empire. As a reserve, he created the Territorial Army – highly trained civilian volunteers who could also move at short notice to support the British army. Meanwhile, the essential part of the defence of the British Empire, the Royal Navy, was being given a very thorough overhaul by Lord Fisher, First Lord of the Admiralty, as it too was dragged into the twentieth century.

Activities

1. How useful are Sources 2.9, 2.10 and 2.11 for investigating the tension between France and Germany? (ENQ)
2. From Source 2.12 and the text, why was it becoming less likely that France would defeat Germany on its own? (KU)
3. According to Sources 2.13, 2.14 and the text, what prevented Britain, France and Russia from becoming friends? (KU)
4. Why did Britain, France and Russia unite against Germany? (KU)

3 Two Armed Camps

F/G The Triple Alliance

In 1871 France was defeated by Germany. Bismarck, then Chancellor of Germany, did not think that peace would last but he knew that France was too weak to fight Germany on her own. To maintain peace he formed alliances to keep France without friends. The most important of these was signed in 1882 when Germany, together with Italy and Austria–Hungary formed a grouping called the Triple Alliance (sometimes called the Central Powers). (See Source 3.1).

Bismarck had also signed an agreement with Russia called a 'Re–insurance Treaty'. In 1891 the Re–insurance Treaty was due to be renewed, but Kaiser Wilhelm II believed he had no need for Russian friendship and so did not renew the Treaty. Russia, like France, now felt alone.

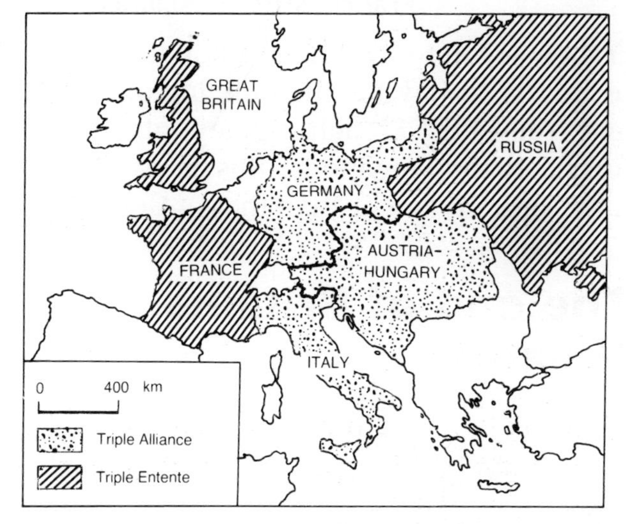

Source 3.1 Europe showing the Great Powers and their alliances in 1907.

Source 3.2 Tsar Nicholas II of Russia blessing his soldiers.

Franco–Russian Alliance

Fear of Germany forced France and Russia together and in 1892 they signed an alliance – the Franco–Russian Alliance. This stated that:

Source 3.3

If France is attacked by Germany, Russia shall use all her forces to attack Germany. If Russia is attacked by Germany, or by Austria supported by Germany, France shall attack Germany.

Franco–Russian Alliance, 1892.

France began to lend large amounts of money to Russia to pay for the building of factories and railways. French money also helped Russia to buy weapons. Russia would soon have an army larger than that of Germany.

The end of Britain's isolation

Unlike France and Russia, Britain did not feel threatened by the Triple Alliance. In fact, the opposite was true:

Source 3.4

In 1892 trouble was expected from France and Russia. The solid, quiet group in Europe was the Triple Alliance of Germany, Austria–Hungary and Italy.

Sir Edward Grey, 1911.

By the end of the nineteenth century Britain was the only Great Power which had not joined an alliance, although she had clearly given it some thought:

Source 3.5

We do not wish to remain permanently isolated in Europe and I think that the natural alliance is between ourselves and the great German Empire.

Joseph Chamberlain, 1898.

However, when Britain wanted to discuss membership of the Triple Alliance with Germany, she was ignored. Then during the Boer War the Kaiser threatened Britain. First he tried to organise an alliance against Britain, then he commanded building to begin on a huge navy for Germany. Britain began to look elsewhere for friends.

The Triple Entente

In 1904, both Britain and France recognised that they feared Germany more than they feared each other. Arguments between the two over their Empires were settled and an agreement was signed in which they promised to cooperate. This agreement, the Entente Cordiale, ended Britain's splendid isolation.

Encouraged by France, Britain and Russia ended their quarrels over colonies (Persia and Afghanistan) and an agreement was signed by all three. This was the Triple Entente.

Source 3.6 A British cartoon on the Entente Cordiale – The caption read 'Let Germany be careful now'.

Two armed camps

By 1908 Europe was firmly divided into two armed camps. On one side stood the Triple Alliance and on the other the Triple Entente. Bismarck's greatest fear had come to pass. The Kaiser's rash actions and threatening manner had united Britain, France and Russia against Germany.

Activities

1. Why had Bismarck kept France without an ally? (KU)
2. What did Russia and France agree to in 1892 according to the evidence in Source 3.3. (KU)
3. According to Sources 3.4 and 3.5 why did Britain consider joining the Triple Alliance? (KU)
4. How can you tell the cartoonist in Source 3.6 supported an alliance between Britain and France? (ENQ)
5. In your own words explain what the 'two armed camps' were. Use the sources and the text to help you. (KU)

C INTERNATIONAL TENSION (1905–1906)

Crisis in Morocco

Stung into action by the signing of the Entente Cordiale in 1904, Kaiser Wilhelm II went to Tangier in Morocco. His government hoped that a crisis over Morocco would revive the traditional hostility towards each other felt by Britain and France. France would see that Britain was an unreliable ally and the Entente Cordiale would be destroyed.

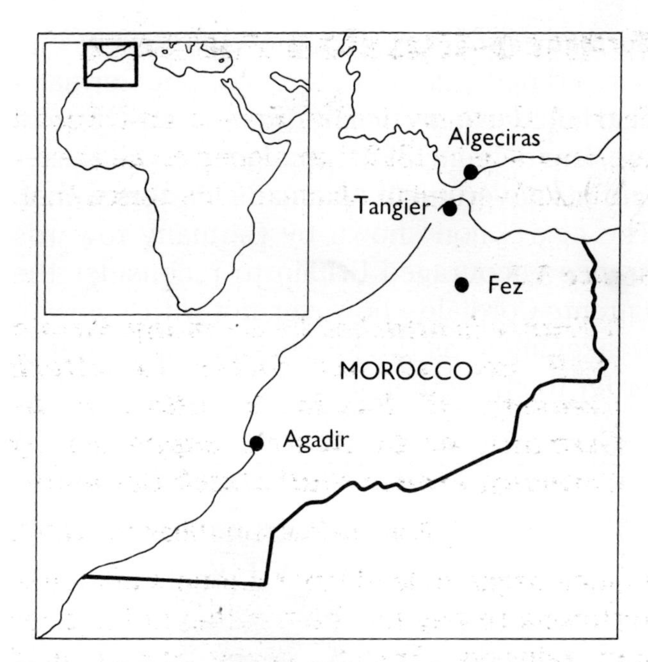

Source 3.7 The Great Powers clashed over Morocco.

The Kaiser's visit was a brief one, just long enough for him to challenge French authority in Morocco in a speech to the Sultan. Morocco should be independent, said the Kaiser, and an international conference must meet to discuss its future. France did not agree.

Source 3.8

> ***Every means was used by Germany to make France understand that if she refused the conference there would be war. France was quite unprepared for war as their army was in a bad state and Russia was unable to help.***

Winston Churchill, 'The Great War', Volume 1.

Under the terms of their alliance of 1892 France could have called on the support of Russia if she was attacked by Germany. However, Germany had timed its move perfectly. In 1905 Russia was defeated in war by Japan and was then paralysed by revolution. France must deal with Germany without her ally. As German threats grew louder, France agreed to a conference. This met in the Spanish town of Algeciras in January 1906. From this point, events turned against

Germany. Not only did the conference support French rights in Morocco, but Germany also failed in her chief purpose: destruction of the Anglo–French Entente. Indeed, the Kaiser and his government had made matters worse. The aggression shown by Germany towards France encouraged Britain to reconsider the Entente Cordiale – however, not with a view to weakening it, as the Kaiser had hoped, but in order to strengthen it.

SOLID.

GERMANY. "DONNERWETTER! IT'S ROCK. I THOUGHT IT WAS GOING TO BE PAPER."

Source 3.9 This Punch cartoon shows German attempts to destroy the Entente Cordiale.

The response by Britain and France was not what Germany expected.

Source 3.10

> ***The Prime Minister authorised the beginning of military conversations between the British and French general staffs with a view to concerted action in the event of war. This was a step of profound significance and of far-reaching importance.***
>
> **Winston Churchill.**

THE MATCH-MAKER MALGRÉ ELLE.

MLLE. LA FRANCE (*aside*). "IF SHE'S GOING TO GLARE AT US LIKE THAT, IT ALMOST LOOKS AS IF WE MIGHT HAVE TO BE REGULARLY ENGAGED."

Source 3.11 Britain and France formed closer links, despite German disapproval.

The Kaiser's unwise actions in 1905–1906 had two major consequences. Firstly France and Britain, who had been on the point of war with each other, settled their differences and began preparing for war against Germany. Secondly, while he had strengthened the Entente Cordiale, the Kaiser had weakened the Triple Alliance. When Italy joined this camp it was on condition that they would never be called upon to fight Britain. So, as friendship grew between Britain and France, Italy and the Triple Alliance began to separate.

Britain and the Triple Entente

As far as Britain was concerned, the Entente Cordiale (published on 8 April 1904) had no military significance. It settled some outstanding colonial problems and nothing more.

The Anglo–Russian Entente, formally concluded on 31 August 1907 is probably of far greater significance. Two years previously these two Powers had been brought to the brink of war with each other in bizarre circumstances. The Russian Baltic fleet was crossing the North Sea bound for the Far East when it received information that hostile Japanese torpedo boats were in the area. This misinformation was allegedly sent by Germany and caused such panic among the Russian crews that when some British trawlers came into view, the warships opened fire. Much to the Kaiser's delight, the British navy shadowed the Russian fleet for several days until a humiliating apology was received from the Tsar.

There then followed the first of the Kaiser's attempts to break up the Entente Cordiale (the second was in Morocco), when he proposed an alliance between Germany and Russia (France's ally) to 'abolish English arrogance and insolence'. Not for the last time, the Kaiser's actions totally failed to achieve the desired outcome. Worried by this erratic and irresponsible behaviour, Britain and Russia resolved their colonial differences and agreed to a new level of diplomatic cooperation. It should be noted however that for Britain this Entente was a sign of its commitment to France rather than Russia. The British public disapproved of the recent sacking of the Russian parliament by the Tsar and the British government had no intention of supporting Russian claims to land in the Balkans.

Britain was also uncomfortable with the term 'Triple Entente' which seemed to suggest a form of alliance which did not exist. As far as Britain was concerned, the Triple Entente had no military meaning. To the leaders of Germany however it seemed that they were being encircled by enemies and it was vital that the army consider how they could successfully fight a war against the Entente Powers.

The Schlieffen Plan

In December 1905 Count Alfred von Schlieffen, the head of the German army, produced a war plan. Since he believed Germany could not win a war on two fronts, he decided not to send his armies to fight in the East and West simultaneously. Instead von Schlieffen planned:

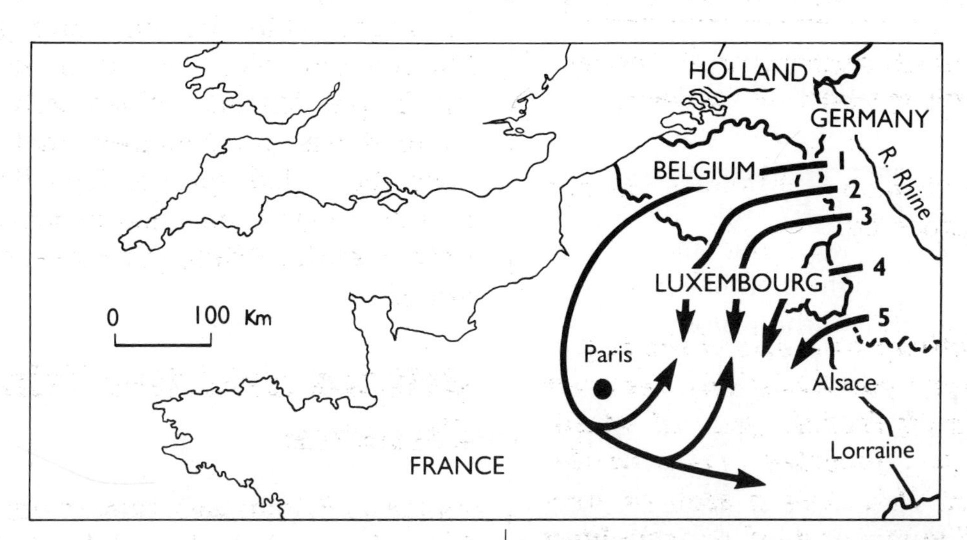

Source 3.12 The Schlieffen Plan (1905) was Germany's plan for winning a war against France and Russia.

Source 3.13

> ***... to hurl the whole of Germany against one opponent, the one who is strongest, most powerful, most dangerous. This cannot be but France-Britain. The Russian army will be unable to march before matters have been decided in the West.***
>
> **Count Alfred von Schlieffen, 1905.**

Von Schlieffen calculated that the Russian army would take six weeks to assemble and he argued that during this lull Germany must crush France. He stressed that speed was essential with the German offensive in the West beginning the moment the Tsar gave the order for the Russian army to mobilise. Von Schlieffen anticipated that French resistance would end when Paris was surrounded and chose what he considered the quickest route to the capital. This meant sending German troops through neutral Belgium and Luxembourg. Here he expected they would encounter the British Expeditionary Force, but their resistance would be token when compared to the chain of French fortresses which blocked more southerly routes. To further aid the rapid movement of the German armies, von Schlieffen drew up a timetable for 11 000 trains. These would carry his men first to the Belgian border and once France had surrendered, they would be used to transfer the German armies to meet the Russian invasion from the east.

Schlieffen's plan was immensely complex and although modified by his successor Count Von Moltke, at least one major flaw remained. A country might mobilise its forces as a warning to a rival, without going to war, as Britain had done in 1911. However, the Schlieffen Plan, dependent on train timetables, once started could not be stopped. Railhead towns such as Aachen (then the size of Dundee) just could not cope with the arrival of 600 000 men. Each army (around 200 000 men) must move out before the next arrived and the Schlieffen Plan dictated that they must move into Belgium and Luxembourg.

Activities

1 Study Source 3.9

a) Describe in detail the incident to which the cartoon refers.

b) What is this source saying about the Entente Cordiale and Germany's reaction to it? (KU)

2 With a partner study Source 3.11.

a) Which countries are represented in this cartoon? (KU)

b) Give two reasons why the elderly lady is looking on in a disapproving manner. (KU)

c) The cartoonist has labelled the elderly lady as 'the matchmaker'. What effect does this suggest her disapproval is having on the couple's relationship? (ENQ)

d) How accurately does this cartoon describe the effects of the Moroccan crisis of 1905? (ENQ)

3 Using Sources 3.8, 3.10, 3.12, 3.13 and the text, how serious a threat to peace were the Kaiser's actions in 1905–1906? (KU)

4 Describe how the Moroccan crisis increased international tension. (KU)

5 **Role Play**: With partner(s), choose one of the following and reenact or write a script for the scene outlined. (KU)

a) Britain, France and Russia discuss why they formed the Triple Entente.

b) Count von Schlieffen and the Kaiser discuss the German war plan.

c) Britain and France discuss the Moroccan crisis.

4 NAVAL RIVALRY

F/G

In 1890, 'Britannia rules the waves' was more than just a line from a song, it was a fact. As an island power with a large overseas empire, Britain depended on the navy for the safety of its trade and empire. It also protected Britain from invasion – especially important when other Great Powers had far larger armies. As Winston Churchill said:

Source 4.1

> ***The purpose of the British navy is purely defensive.***
>
> Winston Churchill, 1914,
> First Lord of the Admiralty.

British control of the seas was not challenged until 1898. In that year, Kaiser Wilhelm II decided to make Germany a naval power, when he declared:

Source 4.2

> ***The future of Germany lies on the water.***

With this announcement, British plans for an alliance with Germany were dropped and these two powers became rivals. Britain would do everything necessary to keep control of the seas. Her policy, often referred to as the 'two power standard', was to have a fleet larger than the next two largest combined. Therefore, when Germany began to build warships rapidly, so too did Britain.

Source 4.3 Admiral Fisher based his battle cruisers directly across the North Sea from Germany.

By 1904, Germany had pulled level with France in the naval race and the Kaiser was calling himself 'Admiral of the Atlantic'. Britain's response was to appoint Sir 'Jackie' Fisher as senior naval officer and he immediately began to reorganise the royal navy.

Perhaps the most important change Fisher introduced was the launch in 1906 of the HMS *Dreadnought*.

Instead of having guns of various sizes, *Dreadnought* only had big guns. While older battleships usually carried four large guns (with barrels of 12 inch diameter), *Dreadnought* had ten. What is more, these were in rotating turrets which meant that they could fire in any direction. She had more armour plating (12 inches thick as opposed to 9) but was also faster than pre-dreadnought ships. Her four steam-driven propellers produced a top speed of 21 knots (nautical miles per hour). Such was the impact of HMS *Dreadnought* that its name became commonly used to describe all ships of a similar type. However, Britain paid a price for introducing this revolutionary warship. It was so much better than the previous types of battleship that it cancelled out Britain's naval supremacy. Now both Britain and Germany raced to build dreadnoughts.

Source 4.4 HMS Dreadnought. This ship could sink an old style navy on its own!

Source 4.5 Dreadnoughts built in Britain and Germany, 1906–1914.

Date	Britain	Germany
1906	1	0
1907	3	0
1908	2	4
1909	2	3
1910	3	1
1911	5	3
1912	3	2
1913	7	3
1914	3	1

The British people were very worried by the building of the German navy. Winston Churchill asked the question on everyone's lips.

Source 4.6

> ***What did Germany want his great navy for? Against whom, except us, could she use it? There was a deep and growing feeling that the Germans meant mischief ... Moreover, we realised that reluctance on our part to build ships would be seen by Germany as a sign of weakness.***
>
> **Winston Churchill, 1933.**

Source 4.7 Britain and Germany raise the stakes in the naval race.

The Kaiser did little to calm British fears. In 1908, with Germany about to increase further the size of its navy, Britain proposed a deal. The Kaiser, however, was in a determined mood:

Source 4.8

If England will only offer the hand of friendship on condition that we limit our navy, it is an absolute cheek, which is a thorough insult to the German people and its Kaiser. If they want war, they can start it, we shall give them what they are asking for!

Kaiser Wilhelm II, 1908.

The Kaiser had already stated why he thought Germany had to have a great navy:

Source 4.9

We must have naval power ... When we have settled our accounts with France and with Russia, will come the the last and greatest settlement of account – with Great Britain.

Kaiser Wilhelm II, 1897.

Activities

1 a) Use the text and Source 4.1. Why was it important for Britain to have a large navy? (KU)
b) How did rivalry between Britain and Germany begin? (KU)

2 Why was HMS Dreadnought an important development for the British navy? (KU)

3 According to Source 4.5, who had won the naval race by 1914? (KU)

4 How does Source 4.7 show the naval rivalry between Britain and Germany? (KU)

5 a) Describe Britain's reaction to the growth of the German navy using Sources 4.3, 4.4, 4.5 and 4.7. (KU)
b) According to Source 4.6, why did Churchill believe that Britain should build ships in competition with Germany? (KU)

6 Read Sources 4.8 and 4.9. Did the Kaiser believe that Germany and Britain would go to war? Give reasons for your answer. (KU)

C 1911–YEAR OF CRISIS

At the beginning of 1911 it was possible for Britain to have rebuilt its friendship with Germany but the Kaiser's actions in that year ended this possibility.

The Kaiser Stirs Hostility

In 1908 Germany launched the first of its Dreadnought-type battleships, *The Westfalen*. This caused great concern in Britain and, when the Kaiser tried to calm British fears, he simply increased them.

Source 4.10 The Westfalen. The launch of this battleship alarmed the British public.

In an interview in the *Daily Telegraph*, the Kaiser said that the English were stupid not to recognise his friendship at a time when most Germans were 'not friendly' to England. This caused an outcry, both in Britain and in Germany. The German Chancellor, von Bulow was bitterly angry at the Kaiser's conduct and offered to resign.

Source 4.11

All the warnings, all the dismal prophecies of the man he had dismissed from office, Bismarck, returned to people's minds. A dark foreboding ran through many Germans that such incautious, over-hasty, stupid, even childish behaviour on the part of the Kaiser could lead only to one thing – catastrophe.

Prince von Bulow, 1908.

The Kaiser was shocked by reactions to his comments and considered abdicating. After this, although naval building went on at pace, there was a period of relative calm. Then, in July 1911, Europe was again plunged into crisis over Morocco.

The Second Moroccan Crisis

Source 4.12

Suddenly and unexpectedly, the German Emperor sent his gunboat **Panther** ***to Agadir, to maintain and protect German interests in Morocco. Great Britain began to wonder what effect a German naval base on the Atlantic coast of Africa would have on her maritime security, her food routes and trade routes. France was genuinely alarmed. It was difficult to work out what was the real purpose behind the German action. Was Germany looking for an excuse for war with France, or merely trying to improve her colonial position?***

Winston Churchil, 1933.

Fearing that the Germans wanted to set up a naval base at Agadir, virtually opposite their vital naval base of Gibraltar, the British government decided on a strong response. A routine confrontation was turned into a war crisis by Britain with the mobilisation of the navy and the delivery of a blistering speech by a leading British politician, David Lloyd George, in which he openly threatened Germany. The German government was stunned by the British reaction not least because Lloyd George was thought to be one of Britain's main peace campaigners.

Results of the Crisis

1 Anglo–German relations worsened.

Faced with the threat of war, the Kaiser had been forced to back down in a humiliating manner and this aroused strong feeling in Germany. It was to Britain that Heydebrand referred when he made the following speech in the German Reichstag:

Source 4.13

> ***Now we know where our enemy stands ... When the hour of decision comes we are prepared for sacrifices, both of blood and of treasure.***
>
> **Heydebrand, 1911.**

This speech was met with thunderous applause. But, while the Kaiser and others shared this view, Admiral Tirpitz insisted that Germany was not yet in a position to force the issue. Once the Kiel Canal was deep enough to allow German Dreadnoughts to pass from the Baltic Sea to the North Sea, then Germany would be ready to challenge Britain. Work on the canal was completed on 23 June 1914.

Source 4.14 Admiral Tirpitz. He insisted that Germany should not go to war until mid-1914.

2 Britain stepped up war preparations.

Britain began to step up its preparations for war against Germany and introduced four significant reforms.

First came the introduction of the 'War Book' which set out the actions each government department should take in the event of war. These actions were sub-divided into a 'Precautionary' and a 'War' stage and would ensure better coordination between the government and the army. In August 1914 the war book was ready.

A second important development in Britain was the founding of the 'intelligence service'. The Second Moroccan Crisis had raised many questions about German foreign policy and so the spy organisations MI5 and MI6 were set up to provide some answers.

Thirdly, the British army's mobilisation procedures (which were frequently practised from 1908) were refined, and railway and shipping timetables were modified to ensure the swift transfer of the army to battle.

Perhaps most significantly of all, Britain and France became much closer. Under the 1912 Anglo–French Naval Convention, the French fleet withdrew to the Mediterranean, while British warships left the Mediterranean for the North Sea. Britain was now obliged to defend the French coast from German attack. As one historian has put it, 'The Entente was coming to look suspiciously like an alliance.'

3 The Franco–Russian Alliance was strengthened.

French patriotism became more intense as a result of the Second Moroccan Crisis, as did French hostility towards Germany. Whereas in the past, French politicians had treated their Russian ally with some reserve, they now told the Russians that they could count on French support against the Triple Alliance no matter how the conflict might start.

4 Balkan tension increased.

The acquisition of Morocco by France had important consequences for world peace. Italy occupied Libya and threatened to invade the Aegean islands. These were part of the Turkish Empire which was in a state of terminal decline. In 1912 the Balkan states took advantage of this crisis by successfully seizing much of what remained of European Turkey. This success went to the heads of the Serbs who began to consider how the 'mighty' Austro–Hungarian Empire might also be overthrown.

Activities

1. What were the main features and the key events of the 'naval arms' race between Britain and Germany? (KU)
2. How far do you agree with von Bulow (Source 4.11) that the Kaiser's actions were 'stupid'. Use the sources and the text to support your answer. (ENQ)
3. Overall, how close to war were Britain and Germany by 1912? Your answer should be in the form of a short essay. (KU)

5 The Balkans

F/G Russia and the Balkans

Turkey had once ruled this corner of Europe, but the Turkish Empire was in decline and new nations, such as Serbia and Bulgaria, had appeared. These countries had won the right to govern themselves and were proud of their independence. But two other great empires wanted to control the Balkans. Rivalry between the Russian Empire and the Austro–Hungarian Empire over the Balkans was a cause of the First World War.

The Russian Empire contained many Slavs and they thought that Russia should protect them in the Balkans. The interest shown in the Balkans by Austria–Hungary was therefore resented. The Russian view was that:

Source 5.1

> ***... In the Balkans there can only be the Turks or ourselves.***
>
> **Serge Sazonov, 1912.**

Source 5.2 'War will come about over some damned foolish thing in the Balkans,' Otto Von Bismarck.

Austria–Hungary and the Balkans

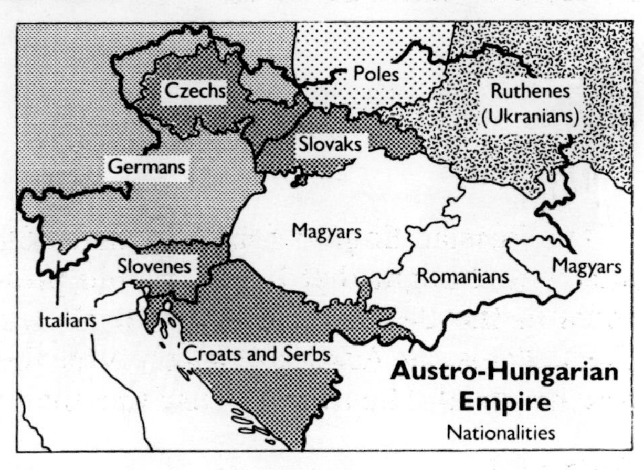

Source 5.3 Austria feared that nationalism would destroy her Empire.

The Austro–Hungarian Empire also contained Slavs, as well as people of ten other nationalities. The Austrians were afraid that these people might copy the nationalists in the Balkans and demand independence. This would destroy the Austro–Hungarian Empire.

It was clear to the Austrian government that the survival of their Empire depended on stamping out nationalism and those who encouraged it. Austria found Slav nationalism most worrying, especially the growing power of Serbia – the largest Slav country. Serbia wanted to govern all Slavs and so hoped to bring the neighbouring lands of Bosnia–Herzegovina under its control. In 1908, these hopes were dashed.

Bosnian crisis 1908

Source 5.4

Austria without warning, took over the Slav provinces of Bosnia and Herzegovina. The Serbians called up their army. But it was the effect on Russia which was most serious. Russians now bitterly hated Austrians and this became a cause of the Great War.

Winston Churchill, 1933, The World Crisis, Volume 1.

Serbia and Russia were angry at Austrian action and both considered going to war with Austria.

Source 5.5

Austria decided that Serbia must accept that Bosnia and Herzegovina were now Austrian. If they did not, then Austria would send an ultimatum and declare war upon her. At this point Germany intervened and insisted Russia should advise Serbia to give way. Russia was to agree to this without informing the British or French governments.

Winston Churchill, 1933.

Faced with this threat, both Serbia and Russia gave in. Both promised that one day they would seek revenge. Germany and Austria were still unhappy. Germany had hoped that this crisis would destroy the Triple Entente but, instead, this agreement had been strengthened. Although they had won, Austria immediately regretted not having taken the opportunity to crush Serbia completely.

Source 5.6 In this French cartoon Austria is shown grabbing Bosnia and Herzegovina. The Bulgarian ruler takes advantage of the confusion to make himself king.

Source 5.7

... as soon as we can, we must settle with Serbia. We can be sure of the Kaiser's support.

Archduke Franz–Ferdinand, 1908.

Source 5.8 Archduke Franz–Ferdinand, heir to the Austrian throne – little did he suspect that it would be his death which would give Austria the excuse to go to war in 1914.

Activities

1 From Sources 5.1, 5.6 and the text, answer the following questions:
a) Who once controlled the Balkans? (KU)
b) Who wanted to control the Balkans? (KU)

2 According to Source 5.3 and the text, why did Austria fear 'nationalism'? (KU)

3 With the help of Sources 5.4 and 5.5, copy and complete the following paragraph: (KU)
In 1908 ______ seized Bosnia and Herzegovina. Serbia reacted by summoning her ______. Russia was also very angry.
At this point ______ stepped in. Germany insisted that ______ should persuade Serbia to give in. Russia was also told not to say anything to her allies who were ______ and ______.

4 Study Sources 5.4, 5.5, 5.7 and the text. How important to Austria was the support of Germany? (KU)

C THE PROLOGUE TO THE FIRST WORLD WAR

Planning the next move

As soon as the Bosnian crisis ended, the military in Germany and Austria began to make plans. In January 1909 the German Chief of Staff, von Moltke, wrote to his Austrian counterpart, Conrad von Hotzendorf:

Source 5.9

The time will come when the patience of Austria–Hungary in the face of Serb provocation will come to an end. Then there will be no alternative but for her to attack Serbia. I can say to you, with the Kaiser's approval, that, if Austria were to attack Serbia and Russia were to mobilise, Germany too would mobilise her whole army, which for her means at once opening hostilities against France and Russia.

Count von Moltke, 1909, German Chief of Staff.

Source 5.10 Conrad von Hotzendorf and Count von Moltke. These were the men who commanded the forces of Austria–Hungary and Germany.

While the military commanders planned, the politicians plotted. The Austrian Chancellor wrote to the German Chancellor von Bulow, in February 1909. He claimed that the Russian people were ready to do anything to avoid war, in which case:

Source 5.11

The idea will be to ensure that any military act against Serbia would not be regarded in Russia as an act of aggression. This, I believe, I can manage by attacking Serbia only when their behaviour becomes openly hostile.

Count Berchtold, 1909.

Source 5.12 Count Berchtold, the Austrian Chancellor.

Berchtold was mistaken to think that Russia would permit an Austrian attack on Serbia. For many years Russia wanted more control over Balkan lands and especially the port of Constantinople. Most Russians believed that it was their duty as the largest of the Slav nations to look after the interests of minority Slav peoples. It hurt them to recall how they had been forced to ignore Bosnian pleas for help against Austria–Hungary. But in 1908 the Russian army had still been recovering from defeat in the Russo–Japanese War and since then steps had been taken to strengthen the army. Russia would not stand aside again but would meet German or Austrian aggression head on and if possible with allies in support.

The Tsar's message to the British government was 'We must keep closer and closer.' Increasingly alarmed by Germany, Britain agreed and in 1914 Britain and Russia held discussions on what military help each could give the other in the event of war.

The Balkan Wars

In 1912 there took place the first European war of the twentieth century when all the Balkan countries (with the exception of Romania) attacked and defeated the Turkish Empire. This war of liberation stirred patriotic emotions and many under age men tried to enlist. One would–be Serb soldier was turned down because he was too young and too feeble. However, this schoolboy would not be denied his place in history – his name was Gavrilo Princip. The Balkan countries were victorious and while Serbia and its allies extended their national boundaries, European Turkey virtually ceased to exist. Predictably, Russia supported the Balkan countries which forced Turkey to look to Germany and Austria–Hungary for help. Britain was quick to get involved. Sir Edward Grey, the British Foreign Minister, organised and chaired a conference of ambassadors in London to keep dialogue going throughout the crisis. This averted war in 1912 but the ultimate showdown still remained in the minds of Europe's leaders. Russia now thought it wise to find out exactly what the terms of their alliance with France meant and in August 1912 Sazonov, the Russian Foreign Minister asked President Poincare to say what France would do if Russia went to war with Germany and Austria–Hungary.

Source 5.13

Poincare emphasised that public opinion in France would not allow his Government to decide on a military action for purely Balkan questions unless Germany intervened. If this happened we shall certainly be able to count on France.

Serge Sazonov, 1912.

Source 5.14 Serge Sazonov (Russian Foreign Minister) and Raymond Poincare (President of France).

The Second Balkan War: The growing threat from Serbia

While Russia and France were agreeing how they would react to the threat of war, Germany and Austria–Hungary were renewing their Alliance. Meanwhile war again broke out in the Balkans. In this war, Serbia again came out best, gaining more territory and doubling in size. Serbia was bigger and stronger in 1913 than it had been in 1908.

Source 5.15

The chances of a victory over Serbia are less favourable for Austria-Hungary than they would have been had we attacked earlier; the one certain thing is that they would grow worse with every year that passed.

Conrad von Hotzendorf, 1913.

In 1913, the Austrian Chancellor, Berchtold, asked for the support of Germany against Serbia. The Kaiser gave the following clear reply:

Source 5.16

If Austria–Hungary demands something, then the Serbian government MUST yield; if it does not, then Belgrade (its capital city) will be bombarded, and occupied. Of this you can be sure, that I stand behind you, and am ready to draw the sword if ever your action makes it necessary!

Kaiser Wilhelm II, 1913.

The Austrian Chancellor observed that, as he spoke, the Kaiser moved his hands towards his sword hilt. This made them feel as if they had been given 'a blank cheque' to do what they wished to Serbia with a guarantee of German support. Meanwhile, Serbia was in confident mood. Having played the leading role in splitting up the Turkish Empire, she now looked towards the Austro–Hungarian Empire. The Serbian Prime Minister Pasitch is reported as having said:

Source 5.17

The first round is won, now we must prepare the second against Austria.

Activities

Group work Form six groups, each to study one of the following countries: Serbia, Austria–Hungary, Germany, Russia, France and Britain.

1 Re-read all relevant Sources and discuss the importance of affairs in the Balkans 1908–1913 for your chosen country. (INV)

2 In your group, write a report on what was discussed. (INV)

3 Report back to the class. (INV)

4 Explain the importance of the Balkans in causing the outbreak of the First World War. (KU)

6 SARAJEVO: THE MURDER THAT ROCKED THE WORLD

F/G

Source 6.1 Franz–Ferdinand and Sophie, his wife, arrive in Sarajevo on the day of the murder.

The plot

On 28 June 1914, Archduke Franz–Ferdinand and his wife visited Sarajevo, in the Austrian province of Bosnia. Crowds lined the streets to watch the royal procession. The Austrian government had promised to take care of security arrangements, but there were few soldiers or policemen around. Along the route were members of a terrorist group called the Black Hand which had its base in Serbia. As the royal car slowed at a junction, one of the terrorists, a 19 year old Serbian called Gavrilo Princip, took his chance.

Source 6.2

I aimed at the Archduke ... I do not remember what I thought at that moment. I only know that I fired twice, or perhaps several times, without knowing whether I had hit or missed.

Gavrilo Princip at his trial, 1914.

Princip's shots were accurate. Both Franz–Ferdinand and his wife were killed. The Archduke's last words were to his wife. He cried, 'Sophie, Sophie, don't die. Live for the sake of the children.'

The lack of security for the royal visit caused comment:

Source 6.3

I had the impression that Archduke Franz Ferdinand was sent on purpose to Sarajevo in the hope that this would provoke an incident which might provide Austria with the excuse for war with Serbia.

Leo Pfeffer, 1914, judge at Princip's trial.

Source 6.4 Franz–Ferdinand's car minutes before the assassination. Barely visible is the number plate A111118, which seems to predict the end of the First World War.

Serbia on trial

Princip admitted his guilt, but this was not enough for the Austrian prosecutor. He intended to prove that the Serbian government was involved. Princip denied this.

Source 6.5 Gavrilo Princip, a Slav nationalist.

Source 6.6

> ***This action was our own idea and in no way official as the prosecution suggests. Serbia had no hand in it. No-one else knew of it.***

Gavrilo Princip, 1914.

Princip must have been convincing because the report of the investigation said:

Source 6.7

> ***There is no proof of the involvement of the Serbian government ... on the contrary, there are grounds for believing it to be quite out of the question.***

But vital evidence had been overlooked. The leader of the Black Hand was the man in charge of the Serbian army. The Serbian government and the Russian government both knew of the plan to assassinate Franz–Ferdinand. But, while the Serbian prime minister had tried to prevent the murders, the Russians had told the Black Hand that they should 'go ahead' and that Serbia 'will not stand alone'.

Reactions

The death of Franz–Ferdinand came as a relief to many Austrians. He was disliked by the Austrian Emperor, the Prime Minister Count Berchtold and many other leading figures. Now Austria had the excuse they wanted to attack Serbia and they had German support. When the Kaiser heard of the assassination he declared:

Source 6.8

> ***Germany is willing ... It is high time a clean sweep was made of the Serbs!***

Kaiser Wilhelm II, 1914.

THE POWER BEHIND.

Source 6.9 This cartoon appeared in 'Punch' on 29 July 1914.

Activities

1. Write a short article for a newspaper in which you describe what happened in Sarajevo on 28 June 1914. (KU)
2. a) Study Sources 6.6, 6.7 and the text. What lies did Princip tell at his trial? (KU)
   b) How successful were his lies? (KU)
   c) Why is Source 6.6 valuable evidence about the assassination. (ENQ)
3. Look at Source 6.9. Did 'Punch' think Serbia had to face Austria alone? Explain your answer. (ENQ)
4. **Group/class discussion**: Who was most to blame for the death of Franz–Ferdinand: Austria, Russia or Serbia? (KU)

C SERBIA IS PUNISHED

Austria was determined to punish Serbia for the crime committed at Sarajevo, but three weeks passed with no action taken. This lack of urgency by Austria annoyed Germany. One government minister, Arthur Zimmermann, urged Austria to 'act without delay' and cursed the amount of time being spelt on 'useless investigations'. The Kaiser, too, insisted that Austria should 'not let the present moment pass'. However, an outright declaration of war by Austria would be considered too strong a reaction by the other Great Powers. Austria had general sympathy and must not lose it. As a first step, therefore, the Austrian government decided to send an ultimatum to Serbia.

Source 6.10 Chancellor Berchtold of Austria gave careful consideration to the wording of the ultimatum.

Source 6.11

Demands must be put to Serbia that would be wholly impossible for them to accept ... A time limit for the reply must be made as short as possible, presumably forty-eight hours, though even this short time limit would be enough for Serbia to get directions from Russia ... Were the Serbs to accept all the demands, this would not be to my liking.

Count Berchtold, 1914.

Meanwhile, this lull had given President Poincare of France the opportunity to visit Russia to discuss the present crisis. Austria went to great lengths to find out Poincare's route.

Source 6.12

Presentation of the ultimatum to Serbia was held back until Monsieur Poincare had left St Petersburg and was once more on the high seas.

HH Asquith, 1923, 'The Genesis of War'.

Source 6.13 President Poincare of France and Tsar Nicholas II of Russia inspect a guard of Russian sailors at St Petersburg, 22 July 1914.

While at sea, the French leader could not be contacted by either the Russian government or his own. The ultimatum could now be sent. Almost at the same moment, the governments of Britain, Russia and France received a note from the German government. This stated that the German government thought that the demands made of Serbia by the Austrian government were:

Source 6.14

... moderate and proper and any interference by Britain, France and Russia would be followed by incalculable consequences.

This threat was issued by the German government before it had seen the text of the Austrian ultimatum. Kaiser Wilhelm, having been sent by his government on a three-week Baltic cruise, knew nothing of these developments. His policies since 1890 had created a recipe for war but by July 1914 he was being pushed aside.

Serbian reply

Serbia accepted eight of the ten points of the ultimatum. This amounted to almost total surrender to Austria. When he finally returned from his cruise, the Kaiser was briefed on recent events. On seeing the text of the Austrian ultimatum, he went white. Alarmed at the Kaiser's reaction, Bethmann-Hollweg offered to resign. The Kaiser refused to allow it saying:

Source 6.15

You have cooked this broth, now you are going to eat it!

Kaiser Wilhelm II, 1914.

Later, when shown a copy of the Serbian reply, the Kaiser's mood changed. He read it enthusiastically:

Source 6.16

> ***A brilliant achievement in a time limit of only forty-eight hours! It is more than one could have expected! A great moral success for Vienna; but with it all reason for war is gone.***
>
> **Kaiser Wilhelm II, 1914.**

Source 6.17 Chancellor Bethmann–Hollweg of Germany. In July 1914 he blocked attempts to prevent the outbreak of war.

The Kaiser then wrote out some ideas which he believed might help prevent war and passed the document to his Chancellor for dispatch. However Herr Bethmann– Hollweg had no intention of carrying out this order – 'Austria will not be denied her victory', he commented. He waited until news came through that Austria had declared war on Serbia before dispatching the Kaiser's peace plan. Of course it was now too late. The avoidable delay to this and to other peace proposals being made at the time, led Sir Edward Grey to comment, 'There's some devilry going on in Berlin.'

On 28 July 1914, exactly one month after the assassination of the heir to their throne, the mighty Austro–Hungarian Empire declared war on Serbia.

Activities

1. According to Sources 6.11, 6.12 and 6.13, how aware was Austria that their ultimatum might lead to war with:
   a) Serbia?
   b) Russia?
   c) France? (KU)
2. How far do Sources 6.12, 6.13 and 6.16 support the view that Germany:
   a) wanted Austria to attack Serbia? (ENQ)
   b) was aware that Russia, France and Britain might become involved? (ENQ)
3. A man of peace or a warmonger? In a group decide which view of the Kaiser is correct. You should also use evidence from earlier work. (INV)
4. Re-read Source 6.16 and the text preceding it in both this and the previous chapter. How consistent is the Kaiser's attitude towards Serbia? (ENQ)
5. How accurate a picture of the Kaiser do we get from Source 6.16 alone? (ENQ)
6. Was Sir Edward Grey correct when he said there was 'some devilry going on in Berlin'? Provide as much evidence as you can to support your view. (ENQ)

7 A WAR THAT NOBODY WANTED

F/G

On 28 July 1914, Austria attacked Serbia. Next day, the Russian army was mobilised to defend Serbia. A Russian diplomat recalled the signing of the mobilisation order.

Source 7.1

The Tsar was deadly pale and spoke in a choking voice.

Maurice Paleologue, 1923, 'An Ambassador's Memoirs' Vol 1.

Austria, now threatened by Russia, looked to her ally Germany for the promised assistance. On 1 August, Germany sent an ultimatum to Russia warning her to cancel moblisation. The deadline was noon but by 4.00 pm Germany had received no reply. Falkenhayn, the German War Minister acted.

Source 7.2

The Chancellor and I drove to see the Kaiser to ask him to sign the mobilisation order. After considerable resistance he consented. Once he had signed, the Kaiser gave me a long hand shake and we both had tears in our eyes.

Erich Falkenhayn, 1914.

The German Ambassador to Russia was then told to deliver the declaration of war. Sazonov, the Russian Foreign Minister, was the man who received it.

Source 7.3

After handing the note to me, the German Ambassador lost all self control and leaning against the window burst into tears.

Serge Sazonov, 1914.

War between Germany and Russia would also involve France, with whom Russia had an alliance. It was against France that Germany struck first. France had to be defeated within six weeks to enable the transfer of the German army to the East to meet the advancing Russians. Germany's declaration of war on France left Britain as the only Great Power not at war. What would Britain do? Britain had signed no alliances and so need not get involved. When Sir Edward Grey was asked by the French Ambassador for help, he replied, 'France must not count on our support.' The German Ambassador also visited him. Grey recalled:

Source 7.4

He was very emotional and begged me not to side with France. He said that Germany, with her army cut in two between France and Russia, was likely to be crushed. He was very agitated, poor man and wept.

Sir Edward Grey, 1914.

Source 7.5 Sir Edward Grey. He warned Germany that Britain would assist France while advising France that she would not.

The invasion of Belgium

Germany pressed on with the attack on France. To achieve a quick victory Germany planned to send troops through Belgium. Belgium was a neutral country wishing only to be left in peace. On 2 August, the German government asked Belgium to allow her troops to pass through. Permission was refused.

On 4 August, German troops poured into Belgium. Britain issued an ultimatum to Germany stating that her troops must leave Belgium by midnight, or Britain would go to war with Germany. Lloyd George described how the British government awaited the German reply.

[Reproduced by permission of the Proprietors of 'Punch.'

BRAVO, BELGIUM!

Source 7.6 A 'Punch' cartoon from August 1914.

Source 7.7

As midnight approached, a deep and tense solemnity fell on the room. No-one spoke. We awaited the signal to send millions of men to their doom. Our eyes wandered anxiously from the clock to the door, and the door to the clock. Boom! the deep notes of Big Ben rang out and a thrill of horror quickened every pulse.

David Lloyd George, 1933, 'War Memoirs' Volume 1.

Meanwhile in Germany, Chancellor Bethmann–Hollweg groaned and said:

Source 7.8

A war that nobody wanted is about to be unleashed.

Chancellor Bethmann–Hollweg, 1915.

Activities

1. Using Sources 7.1 and 7.2 compare the reactions of the Tsar of Russia and the German Kaiser to the outbreak of war. (ENQ)
2. Sources 7.1 and 7.7 give the same reason why Europe's leaders were upset at this time. What is this reason? (KU)
3. Source 7.7 describes the British government awaiting a message.
   a) From whom? (KU)
   b) What did the government hope the message would say? (KU)
4. Source 7.3 mentions one person who wept when war was declared. Identify three others from other Sources who did the same. (KU)

Group work

5. Give reasons why Source 7.6 is a useful source for those studying the outbreak of the First World War. (ENQ)
6. Discuss how far you agree with Bethmann–Hollweg (Source 7.8) that the war now breaking out was 'a war that nobody wanted'. (ENQ)

C BRITAIN MUST BE HELD RESPONSIBLE?

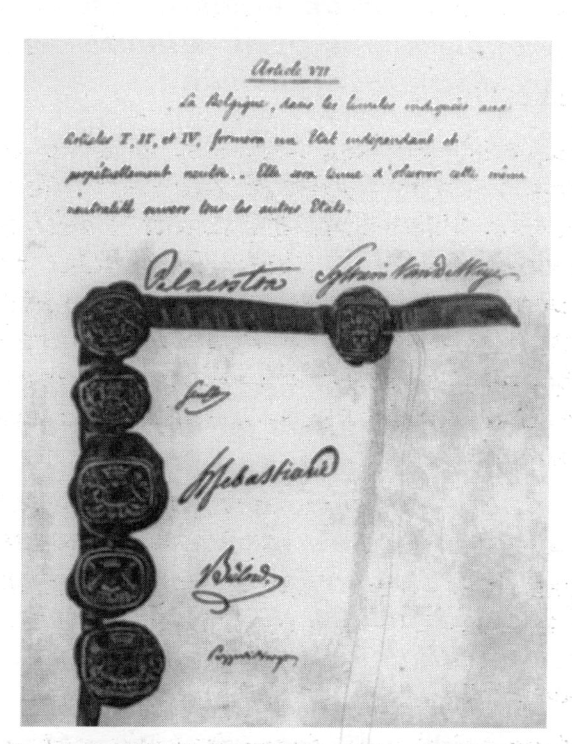

Article VII

La Belgique, dans les limites indiquées aux Articles I, II, et IV, formera un État indépendant et perpétuellement neutre. Elle sera tenue d'observer cette même neutralité envers tous les autres États.

Palmerston

Source 7.9 The Treaty of London 1839. Britain was one of the signatories.

By signing the Treaty of London, Britain had promised to defend Belgian neutrality, even if that meant going to war. Germany thought Britain was taking this far too seriously, as Bethmann–Hollweg explained to the British Ambassador:

Source 7.10

Just a word – 'neutrality', a word which in war-time had so often been disregarded – just for a scrap of paper, Great Britain was going to make war on a kindred nation who desired nothing better than to be friends with her . . . what Britain had done was unthinkable; it was like striking a man down from behind whilst he was fighting for his life against two assailants. Britain must be held responsible for the terrible events that might happen.

Bethmann–Hollweg, 1914.

Strong feelings were aroused in Britain over the German invasion of neutral Belgium. To many it was not the act of a civilised nation. German hostility to Britain was equally strong. Many leading Germans had not expected Britain to become involved in the war. The Kaiser felt he had been deceived. 'The low down shopkeeping knaves,' he said, 'have been trying to take us in.' Falkenhayn, the German War Minister declared:

Source 7.11

Of course we never expected for one moment that Britain would enter the war ... the coming in of Britain made all the difference in the world.

Erich Falkenhayn, 1914.

When Bethmann–Hollweg learned of Britain's intention to support France and Russia, he immediately contacted the Austrian government:

Source 7.12

In these circumstances we most urgently and emphatically recommend that you settle the dispute with Serbia, or else we will face catastrophe.

Bethmann–Hollweg, 1914.

Admiral Tirpitz was another who felt that Germany would have done more to preserve the peace if they had known sooner that Britain might become involved.

Source 7.13

Britain brought upon itself a large share of the responsibility for the outbreak of the war by uncertainty as to its attitude during the crisis. Grey could have preserved peace if he had in time made clear to Bethmann–Hollweg Britain's attitude in the event of the Austro–Serbian conflict spreading to the rest of Europe.

Alfred von Tirpitz, 1919, 'My Memoirs'.

This view is also supported by Sazonov.

Source 7.14

A decisive statement on the part of the British government of its solidarity with France had in 1911 been sufficient to dispel the gathering storm clouds. I am convinced now that, had the British government sided with Russia and France on the Serbian question from the first, Berlin would not have encouraged Austria in its policy of aggression but would, on the contrary, have advised caution and moderation.

Serge Sazonov, 1927, 'Fateful Years'.

Winston Churchill was of the same opinion:

Source 7.15

Our Entente with France and the military and naval conversations that had taken place since 1906 had given us the obligations of an alliance without its advantages. An open alliance would have discouraged Germany.

Winston Churchill, 1933,
'The World Crisis' Volume 1.

However, this view was not shared by two people at the centre of events:

Source 7.16

There is no evidence to prove that a threatening attitude on our part would have turned Germany and Austria from the path on which they had entered. On the contrary the evidence is all the other way. Bethmann–Hollweg himself has ridiculed the idea that Germany made a miscalculation in counting on British neutrality.

Herbert Asquith, British Prime Minister
(1908–1915), 'The Genesis of War', 1923.

Source 7.17 A 'Punch' cartoon from 1914.

In the Europe of 1914, too few people dreaded the prospect of war. In Russia, and in Austria–Hungary, there were those who saw war as a way to avoid revolution at home. In France, many shared the opinion that never before had war offered itself under such favourable conditions. In Germany, as far back as December 1912, it was decided that the war could begin against the Entente Powers sometime after 23 June 1914. This was the expected date for completion of improvements to the Kiel Canal. It was not only the German navy which favoured war in 1914, but also the army:

Source 7.18

> ***The situation is from the military point of view, favourable to a degree which cannot occur again in the foreseeable future.***
>
> **Helmuth von Moltke,**
> **German Chief of Staff, 1914.**

By midnight on 4 August 1914, those who wanted war had their wish. Sir Edward Grey commented, 'The lamps are going out all over Europe. They will not be lit again in our lifetime.'

Activities

1 Compare the cartoons in Sources 7.6 and 7.17

a) In what ways are they similar? (ENQ)

b) In what ways is cartoon 7.17 more critical of Germany? (ENQ)

c) How could Germany claim to be defending itself? (KU)

2 Role play

Form six groups. Each group is to represent one of the following countries: Germany, Austria–Hungary, Russia, France, Britain and Serbia. Each group should study the attitudes and actions of their country in the years before 1914. Each group in turn should make a confession to the class concerning their role in bringing about the First World War. Once each confession has been made, the class can discuss each claim and attribute blame. (INV)

8 THE FIRST EXPERIENCE OF WAR – ATTITUDES IN 1914

F/G

Source 8.1 An excited crowd gathered in Trafalgar Square on 4 August to welcome the coming of war.

On 4 August 1914, a young English girl called Vera Brittain noted this in her diary.

Source 8.2

> ***I am almost too excited to write at the stupendous events of this day – war is declared between France and Germany. Sir Edward Grey's statement that 'we are prepared' got a tremendous cheer in the House (of Commons).***
>
> Vera Brittain, 'Testament of Youth'.

Later that day as the German invasion of Belgium continued, the British Government under Prime Minister Henry Asquith, declared war on Germany and took Britain into the war. All over Europe there was great excitement when war was declared – after all there had not been a major war in Europe for nearly 100 years and in Britain the declaration was greeted with great enthusiasm. Crowds took to the streets waving flags and singing patriotic songs. People danced and cheered outside Buckingham Palace in a wave of patriotism which swept the country in those first days of the war.

Britain though, was only partly ready to fight a war. Britain's strength had always been in its navy but its army was small. Lord Kitchener, British Secretary of State for War, believing that the war would be a long one declared:

Source 8.3

> ***... three years will do to begin with. A nation like Germany, will only give in after it is beaten to the ground. That will be a very long time. No-one living knows how long.***

Lord Kitchener, 1914.

This view, though, was not popular. Instead, the newspapers preferred to encourage the belief that it would be a short war – over by Christmas at the latest.

Government action – recruitment

When war broke out a British Expeditionary Force (BEF) was mobilised and within a week about 80 000 professional British soldiers had been sent across the channel. Kitchener realised that for a long war, the army had to be enlarged and so he called for 100 000 volunteers to form a second army. One of the earliest experiences of war for young British men was to be bombarded with Government propaganda aimed at persuading them to volunteer for Kitchener's new army.

Source 8.4 The posters encouraged enlistment through patriotism.

Patriotism

Young men were put under great pressure by families and friends to join up. Posters like Sources 8.4 and 8.5 began to appear and it was soon a disgrace for a young man to be seen in the streets without a uniform. Later in the war there was a campaign by women to disgrace men not in uniform by pinning a white feather (a sign of cowardice) to their jackets.

Source 8.5 The call to 'Do your duty' was a powerful influence on young men.

The call to the nation for volunteers was a huge success. Pride and patriotism combined to persuade over 500 000 young men to join the army in the first weeks of the war.

Activities

Copy and complete questions 1–3

1. Britain declared war on ________ because ________________(KU)
2. The people of Britain were ________ about going to war. I know this from Sources 8.1 and 8.2 because ______ ________________________(KU)
3. The B ______ E ______ F ______ was sent to France in 1914. (KU)
4. Why did Britain need to raise a large army in 1914? Use Source 8.3 and the text to help you find two reasons. (KU)
5. In what way did the poster in a) Source 8.4 and b) Source 8.5 encourage young men to enlist? (ENQ)
6. What evidence is there that the Government's recruitment campaign was a success? (KU)

C TAKING THE 'KING'S SHILLING'

Source 8.6 A British poster during the First World War.

Propaganda

On the outbreak of the war, the Government launched a propaganda campaign to encourage enlistment. Terrible acts of cruelty by the Germans were reported in the British Press – stories of mothers and their children being bayonetted by German soldiers and of innocent villagers being shot without reason were printed. The Germans were portrayed as beasts and brutal murderers who slaughtered innocent women and children. Most of these stories were inventions of British newspapers which were determined to whip up as much anti-German feeling as possible, but they did succeed in persuading many British men to fight.

There were other reasons for joining up in 1914. According to Robert Graves:

Source 8.7

> ***The papers predicted only a very short war – over by Christmas at the outside.***
>
> **Robert Graves, 'Goodbye to All That'.**

Graves also preferred to join up rather than go to University. His generation was persuaded by music hall entertainers, posters, bosses, parents, friends and families that joining the army was the right thing to do, and the young men of 1914 flocked to the recruiting stations in huge numbers.

Such was the excitement in the opening weeks of the war that many young men enlisted because their pals had joined up and they didn't want to be left out. Amongst the recruits, however, were many who should not really have been accepted. Some were even prepared to trick their way in. One would-be recruit, George Coppard, was encouraged to lie by the recruiting sergeant in order to be allowed to enlist:

Source 8.8

> ***The sergeant asked me my age and when told, replied, 'Clear off son. Come back tomorrow and see if you're nineteen.' So I turned up again the next day and gave my age as nineteen. ... I was sixteen years and seven months old.***
>
> **George Coppard, 'With a machine-gun to Cambrai'.**

Stories of boys and men enlisting in this way were common throughout the country. In some areas, whole streets of men volunteered together so they could serve with their friends. In Glasgow, the Corporation tramcar drivers and conductors joined as a group and became the 15th Highland Light Infantry. The 16th Highland Light Infantry was the Glasgow Boys' Brigade. The Heart of Midlothian football team also joined up as a unit in the 16th Royal Scots. These 'Pals' Battalions' went off to train together for their turn at the front, but later events on the Somme in 1916 were to show just what a tragic mistake it was to allow so many from the one neighbourhood to join the same battalion.

Source 8.9 Enlistment by a hairsbreadth! The army frequently stretched the rules.

The army accepted many volunteers who should not have been accepted – but the army needed manpower in 1914. However, when they joined, the volunteers could not be turned into soldiers overnight and many could not even be provided with uniforms or a rifle. To begin with, these members of 'Kitchener's Army' drilled in their ordinary clothes and carried sticks or broom handles for rifles. Throughout 1915 the training continued and by early 1916 they were finally ready to take their part in the war to replace the territorials and regular army soldiers who had become casualties on the western front.

Source 8.10 German students celebrate the declaration of war.

European war fever

War fever had gripped Britain but the excitement and enthusiasm for battle was the same throughout Europe. French, Belgians, Germans, Russians and Austrians all marched to war believing in the glory of their cause. All over Europe young men joined their national armies fully believing that they were being called to defend their country from the aggression of others. On 6 August 1914, a young German student wrote to his mother.

Source 8.11

> ***My dear ones, be proud that you live in such times and in such a nation, and that you have the privilege of sending several of those you love into this glorious struggle.***
>
> **Walter Limmer, 1914.**

Activities

1. Compare the views of Kitchener (Source 8.3) and Graves (Source 8.7) about the length of the war. Whose prediction was most likely to be accurate and why? (ENQ)
2. How typical is Source 8.6 as an example of anti-German propaganda. Look for other examples in this book. (ENQ)
3. Explain why young men joined the army. (KU)
4. Why do you think George Coppard cheated to get into the Army? (KU)
5. Compare the attitudes towards the declaration of war in Britain and Germany. (ENQ)
6. **Class discussion:** What were the reasons why the British Government's recruitment campaign was so successful in 1914? (INV)
   You should consider the following – patriotism, propaganda, predictions in the papers, poster campaign, patriotic songs, peer pressure.
7. Write a short essay describing the recruitment campaign and the reasons for its success. (KU)

9 MODERN WARFARE

F/G When war broke out in 1914 the generals of all sides expected a war of movement. It was thought that cavalry and infantry charges would destroy the enemy and that victory would be swift. Having masses of men was considered an advantage and it was thought that Russia's millions in the east would crush the Germans like a steamroller.

In the west, the French plan to attack the Germans, Plan 17, relied upon the cavalry and infantry. Before 1914, General Haig (who was later to become the Commander of the British Army), had predicted ...

Source 9.1

> ***The cavalry will have an important role in future wars.***
>
> **General Douglas Haig, 1914.**

Events were to prove him very wrong.

Source 9.2 The machine-gun made infantry and cavalry charges across open ground suicidal.

The impact of new technology

Source 9.3 The modern battlefield.

By 1914 new technology had been developed for modern armies – big guns capable of accurate shellfire over long distances and machine-guns which were able to fire hundreds of bullets every minute – but it was the Germans who had . . .

Source 9.4

> ***studied the machine-gun more than other armies and were able to use its power to dominate a battlefield sooner than other armies.***

B Liddell-Hart, 1970, 'History of World War I'.

The French soldiers of 1914 went into battle wearing brightly coloured uniforms. Their tactics were to charge towards the German positions courageously with their bayonets at the ready. However, on the fields of Alsace and Lorraine, they were easy and colourful targets for German machine-gunners. They were slaughtered in huge numbers. The British and French were slower to understand the power of the machine-gun, some believing it to be . . .

Source 9:5

> ***a much over-rated weapon and two per battalion is more than enough.***

General Douglas Haig, 1914.

The power of the machine-gun

At the start of the war the generals were wrong in how they believed the war would develop. Too many of them still thought that the sabre (sword) of the horseback soldier, the bayonet of the footsoldier coupled with grit and determination would win wars. Too few of them had learned the lessons of previous wars in which the increasing power of weapons had changed the nature of warfare. Judge for yourself the power of the machine-gun from this incident which took place in 1916.

Source 9.6

> ***The front line jumped up and walked into the open ... machine-guns from several points sprayed their deadly fire backwards and forwards dropping men like corn before the reaper. In far less time than it takes to write it, the attacking waves became a mere sprinkling of men. They went on for a yard or two and then all seemed to vanish.***

Captain Gilbert Nobbs, July 1916.

Until the realities of modern warfare became obvious, the generals had all been sure that a swift victory could be achieved and that the enemy would soon be crushed – modern fire-power destroyed their hopes.

Activities

1. One of the soldiers in Source 9.3 is French, one German and one British. By using Sources 9.1, 9.2 and 9.4 and the text identify each soldier correctly. (ENQ)
2. Imagine the diagram showed a real event. Which of the soldiers would have the best chance of survival. Give two reasons for your answer. (KU)
3. Use Source 9.3 to help you:
   a) If soldiers had to 'dig in' before attacking towards machine-gunners this would lead to long/short battles. (Choose one of the underlined words.) Give at least one reason for your answer. (KU)
   b) If soldiers attacked machine-gunners in large numbers there would probably be large/small numbers of casualties. (Choose one of the underlined words.) Give one reason to explain your answer. (KU)

C MODERN FIREPOWER

Source 9.7 The armies of 1914 were supported by artillery fire from guns which increased in size and effectiveness like this 30.5cm heavy German siege howitzer.

The war of movement

In August 1914 Germany launched an attack against France, following closely the plan laid down by von Schlieffen in 1905 with a massive force which advanced through Belgium. The German advance depended on three factors – the power of the artillery, the speed of their cavalry and the sheer weight of numbers of their infantry soldiers. However, from the beginning they encountered problems. For 18 vital days their advance was delayed by the Belgian army which was outnumbered by almost a hundred to one but who fought with desperation until they could fight no more. The Germans faced the might of modern fire-power at Liege in Belgium where their advance was halted by a hail of machine-gun fire until they lay . . .

Source 9.8

heaped one on top of the other in an awful barricade of dead and wounded. It was slaughter – just slaughter.

J Terraine, 'White Heat'.

By 20 August though, the Belgians were forced to retreat to Antwerp. The Germans entered Brussels as conquerors and the German army once again pushed forward into northern France. By 20 August the British Expeditionary Force (BEF) was in Belgium and their first action against the Germans took place on the Mons to Brussels road. A troop of mounted Dragoon Guards came across a unit of the German cavalry. In the skirmish that followed the Germans were scattered and at least one was killed – but despite setbacks like this, the German advance continued relentlessly. At Mons and at Le Cateau the BEF fought desperately to try to stop the German advance, but as the weight of numbers began to tell the BEF and the French armies were forced to fall further and further back.

Both sides by now were using aircraft for reconnaissance and as they surged forward German pilots gave their gunners invaluable information pinpointing the positions held by the British and French. The German artillery pounded their defensive positions time after time forcing the defenders to dig themselves in to ditches in the ground for some protection. All too often the weight of the attack was too great and the defenders were forced to retreat in the face of the onslaught of shrapnel and high explosive.

The BEF and the French armies retreated until they reached the River Marne where in early September 1914 they halted. All along the front the French and British regrouped and counter–attacked. With their plan now having failed, the Germans decided to withdraw to a strong defensive line and to hold on to what they had gained. They pulled back to the River Aisne and dug deep trenches which they protected with coils of barbed wire. Gradually the line of trenches was extended as each side tried to outflank the other until they stretched from the English Channel in the north to Switzerland in the south.

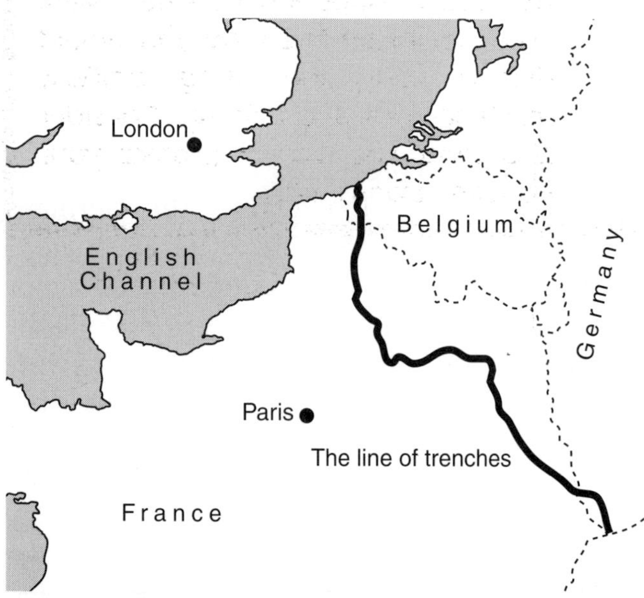

Source 9.9 Between September and November the two armies gradually established trench lines facing each other from the English Channel to the Swiss border.

The new battlefield

The hail of fire which swept the modern battlefield had proved devastating to soldiers on open ground. The soldiers of 1914 faced a battlefield full of flying metal, and battles had pitted men against machines. Men in the open could not survive. The crude shells burst into large, jagged chunks of hot metal causing the most horrifying woulds. It was not uncommon for a soldier to be sliced in two by a shell fragment. Nor was it unusual to find shattered pieces of body lying on the battlefield – legs, arms and even heads separated from the torso. The safety of a man came to depend more on his handling of a spade than his rifle as the deeper he dug, the better was his shelter from flying metal. The spade now became the key to safety as troops from all of the warring nations dug trenches to protect themselves from the effects of modern technology. In the new warfare of machine–guns, rifles and artillery it was much easier to defend than it was to attack. The day of the mounted cavalryman and the bayonet charge of the infantryman was at an end. New technology changed the character of the war.

Casualties

By September 1914 the various war plans had failed in the face of modern firepower – the French Plan 17, the German Schlieffen Plan, the Russian 'Steamroller' – and all of them had ended with enormous casualties. French losses by the end of August 1914 were a staggering 211 000 officers and men either dead or wounded. German casualties were as bad if not worse as they were fighting on two fronts, in France and in Russia. The BEF had fought with enormous gallantry against heavy odds but it too had suffered frightening casualties in the face of the new technology.

By the end of 1914 the BEF was holding the line close to the English Channel in Belgium and into northern France.

Source 9.10

We are now in billets 20 miles behind Ypres ... Well you may know that out of the 1100 officers and men that came out here at the start we have Major Yeadon and about 80 men left.

Corporal George Matheson, 1st Battalion The Queen's Own Cameron Highlanders, November 1914.

Since engaging the Germans in August the BEF had suffered 90 per cent casualties – killed, wounded and missing. It had ceased to exist as a fighting force.

Stalemate

The war of movement was now at an end and the rival armies found themselves in parallel rows of trenches separated by a belt of disputed territory known as 'no-man's land' – in some places a thousand yards wide, in others only a few yards.

Source 9.11 Parallel rows of trench lines separated by no-man's land as seen from the air. Barbed wire prevented soldiers reaching enemy trenches.

The generals of both sides were faced with this problem: there could be no victory without forward movement, but forward movement without high casualties was impossible. For the next four years the generals of the rival armies struggled to find the key to breaking through the enemy lines and ending trench warfare.

Activities

1 **Class discussion**: What was the role and importance of each of the following in the first four months of the war? (KU)
   a) Artillery
   b) Machine-gun
   c) Aircraft
   d) Spade
2 What evidence is there that the new form of warfare was very destructive? (KU)
3 What developments made it easier for an army to defend rather than to attack? (KU)
4 Sketch part of a battlefield showing two sets of opposing trenches. Mark and explain on this how you would defend your line using artillery, machine-guns and infantry. Consider also how you would protect your front-line troops. (KU)

10 LIFE IN THE TRENCHES

F/G The trenches

Source 10.1 The trenches were six or seven feet deep and the front and rear were strengthened with sandbags. Dug-outs were dug into the sides of the trenches for extra shelter.

The British view of trenches was summed up by George Coppard.

Source 10.2

> ***Our trench warfare seemed to be based upon the idea that we were not stopping in the trenches for very long, and that very soon we would be chasing Jerry across country. The result was that we lived a mean and impoverished sort of existence in lousy scratch holes.***
>
> George Coppard, 'With a machine-gun to Cambrai'.

Instead of temporary trenches, the Germans built a strong network of trench lines because they were on enemy soil and were determined to hold on to the land they had won.

Conditions at the front

The trench system proved so difficult to break through that the soldiers of both sides were camped opposite each other for four years. Living outdoors in all weathers in summer and in winter was uncomfortable and unpleasant. When the ground was torn up by constant artilleryfire, conditions simply got worse and worse.

Source 10.3

Flanders is just one great bog. Day and night we stand up to our knees in mud and water. On top of this, the mad gun-battle goes on in front of us and it is dangerous even to raise your head above ground during the day.

Friedrich Nickolas, December 1915.

Source 10.4 The dirt and filth of the trenches encouraged rats and lice. 'Corpse rats' fed on the bodies of dead soldiers.

When they were 'in the line' the soldiers faced other problems as well as enemy fire. In areas where the trenches were muddy and full of water the soldiers had to spend a great deal of their time in working parties getting rid of the water.

Source 10.5

We took turns in one part of the trench bailing out water with a bucket. One morning, a man named Davies had his thumb shot off whilst bailing. The next man deliberately invited a bullet through his hands by exposing them a little longer than necessary – but the bucket got riddled instead.

Frank Richards, from 'Old soldiers never die'.

Standing in water and squelching mud for long periods was uncomfortable and many soldiers got a condition known as 'trench feet' when their feet swelled and became very painful. This occasionally led to soldiers having to have their feet amputated.

Winter conditions were especially bad and it was not unknown for soldiers to be in tears with the cold. Sentry duty involved staying awake all night in freezing temperatures and was enough to test the endurance of any man. For others trying to get some sleep in the freezing conditions it was equally bad. One soldier in the front line on a winter's night got a fright when he woke up. He couldn't move and thought he was paralysed. The greatcoat he was wearing had been wet and had frozen stiff during the night!

Rations

The most dangerous times of the day for the soldiers at the front were dusk and dawn, for these were the favourite times for raids by the enemy. For a time before it got dark at night and before it got light in the morning sentries had to 'stand to' – that is, be on the look-out for enemy patrols attacking their trenches. When the danger time was passed both armies settled down, in the morning to breakfast and in the evening to supper.

The soldiers at the front had to be fed and every battalion had a quartermaster whose job it was to ensure that their soldiers got food and drink. For the majority of the time the basic diet was tinned 'bully beef' washed down with tea. On some mornings, however, the smell of bacon and eggs wafted across no-man's land as both sets of soldiers settled to breakfast at the start of another routine day in the trenches.

Source 10.6 Soldiers of the Royal Scots Fusiliers endure the misery of the trenches in Flanders, 1915. Donald Snaddon (Source 1.1) served with this regiment.

Contact with home

While in the trenches soldiers received letters and parcels from home. These often contained socks, scarves and woollen hats to keep the soldiers warm but there were also treats like cakes and biscuits sent by concerned mums to their sons in the front line. The soldiers were allowed to write home to their families but their letters and cards were all censored by the military authorities to ensure that no important information was given away. However, the contact with home was a comfort to the soldiers fighting in the front line.

Routine work

A soldier could usually expect to be in the front line for a week to ten days at a time during 'quiet times' before going to the rear for rest. There were many jobs which had to be attended to by these soldiers. During the summer soldiers had to cut the grass which grew in front of their trenches amongst the barbed wire, because the long grass obscured the view of sentries. This was a dangerous job as it had to be done out of the safety of the trenches and it was normally done at night. However the least sound could attract a burst of fire from the enemy trenches by a sniper or a machine-gunner. Damaged trenches and wire had to be repaired constantly. This was often dangerous work as snipers were always on the lookout for unwary soldiers. A British soldier, Frank Bastable recalled the story in Source 10.7, about the death of his friend Bill Beckington in August 1915.

Source 10.7

We hadn't been in the line long. Bill and I were told to go up and repair a trench. When we got there he said, 'I'll go up. You fill the bags and hand them up to me.' But as soon as he went up there was a shot and Bill was hit in the head. I can still see it now, bits of his brains on my tunic. Poor Bill, they should have told us.

Frank Bastable, 'The Somme'.

Source 10.8 German sniping team with spotter and killer.

Life in the front line trenches was uncomfortable and dangerous. For some soldiers the strain was too much and soldiers of both sides sometimes gave up. A British officer came across this man in a dug-out:

Source 10.9

I shook him by the arm and noticed a hole in the back of his head. He had taken off the boot and sock to pull the trigger of his rifle with one toe; the muzzle was in his mouth.

Robert Graves, 'Goodbye to all that'.

Source 10.10 The German artist Otto Dix shows that Germans also committed suicide.

Activities

1. Which of the Sources agree that:
   a) it was dangerous to raise your head above ground level.
   b) trench warfare was too much for some soldiers. (ENQ)
2. Why are eyewitness accounts useful to historians studying conditions in the trenches?
   Consider a) who the authors were b) whether the Sources agree about conditions; c) the photographic evidence. (ENQ)
3. Describe a typical front line trench. (KU)

C TRYING TO BREAK THE DEADLOCK

10.11 Sitting still would not win the war.

From November 1914 the war bogged down into trench stalemate. In the west, the lines of trenches stretched from the Belgian coast to Switzerland making it impossible for any of the generals to outflank their enemies. With the onset of winter, the opposing armies settled down to regroup and to gather their strength in the hope that 1915 would see the breakthrough which would lead to the end of the war.

For Britain and France the simple truth was that the war could not be won by remaining in the trenches while the Germans were camped on French and Belgian soil. It was essential to remain on the offensive, but the barbed wire and the machine-guns meant that frontal assaults on trench positions were certain to lead to high casualties. New methods of successfully attacking the enemy trenches had to be found. During the next four years more and more sophisticated ways were tried in an effort to end the deadlock including artillery bombardments, tanks, underground mines and poison gas.

Technology: artillery – the 'God of War'

With the war bogged down in trenches, the biggest stumbling block was the barbed wire and the deadly fire of the machine-guns. However, while the trench lines remained fixed it was possible to use large immobile guns against the enemy positions and to concentrate fire along short sections of the front line. The first to use this tactic in May 1915 was General Ferdinand Foch, who launched an offensive in Artois towards Vimy Ridge which was held by the Germans. Before he committed his infantry to battle, Foch ordered a massive bombardment of the enemy positions to soften up the German defenders and to destroy the wire. From then onwards, artillery was to become the 'God of War' and was used before almost every major offensive.

In 1916 the artillery bombardment took on a more sinister aspect as the German General von Falkenhayn attempted to break the deadlock at the French town of Verdun.

Operation 'Gericht'

Verdun was a strongpoint in the French defences as it was surrounded by a ring of fortresses. For historical reasons it was also a place which the French considered too precious to lose. General von Falkenhayn realised that the French would attempt to hold on to Verdun at all costs.

Source 10.12

> ***Within our reach behind the French sector of the Western front there are objectives for the retention of which the French General Staff would be compelled to throw in every man they have. If they do so the forces of France will bleed to death.***

Erich von Falkenhayn, 1916.

Falkenhayn launched a massive artillery attack on Verdun in February 1916 to draw the French army in to its defence and to 'bleed it to death'. In total he concentrated 1220 guns to attack a front of barely eight miles. Also, aircraft were used to support ground tactics. 168 planes, and four Zeppelins were mustered for the attack. Their role was to protect the vital observation balloons from attack by the French, thus allowing the gunners to have a stream of accurate information from their observers.

Falkenhayn's plan to wear down the French numbers deliberately, by sucking them in to defend Verdun and then to destroy them by artillery fire was called attrition.

Attrition

On 21 February 1916 the German bombardment opened. The whole day guns rained down a hail of shells into the French forward areas and the following morning as the survivors struggled out from what little shelter they had found they did not recognise the landscape. Trees had been uprooted and smashed to pieces. From the stumps which remained hung shredded uniforms with the gruesome fragments of soldiers who had been blown apart. The ground had been torn up and was pitted with enormous shellholes made by some 80 000 heavy shells which had fallen in a rectangle only 500 metres by 1000 metres.

The experience of being under a bombardment was described by Paul Dubrulle who served at Verdun.

Source 10.13

> ***To die from a bullet seems to be nothing; but to be dismembered, torn to pieces, reduced to pulp, this is a fear that flesh cannot support and which is the great suffering of the bombardment.***

Another, Sergeant-Major Cesar Melera described the feelings he had under bombardment.

Source 10.14

> ***Verdun is terrible .... because man is fighting against material with the sensation of striking out at empty air.***

Both quoted from 'The Price of Glory – Verdun 1916' by Alistair Horne.

The slaughter continued without respite throughout the spring and summer of 1916 but the French held Verdun. During the course of the battle over 1000 shells were fired for every square metre of the battlefield and the total casualties for the battle was over 700 000 – the French suffering slightly more than the Germans. Falkenhayn's plan had been partially successful, but he had allowed too many Germans to be drawn into the attempted capture of Verdun. The campaign of attrition almost bled dry not only the French but also the German army. The big guns then, despite their power, could not win a quick decisive victory. Attrition, wearing down the enemy's numbers, would be a slow process and was bound to lead to ever increasing casualty lists.

Counter measures

There was little protection against the big guns except to dig down deeper and deeper. In some sectors along the Western Front as, for example at the Somme, dug-outs were as deep as 9–12 metres and reinforced with concrete. To counter the effects of shrapnel the soldiers of all armies were eventually issued with steel helmets since a very high percentage of deaths occurred from head wounds.

In the meantime, the new British army was about to be called into action for the first time. On 24 June 1916 the British army opened up its own massive artillery bombardment along a 14 mile front in Picardy astride the River Somme.

Source 10.15 The increasing use and concentration of the guns.

Date	Battle	Heavy Guns	Front (miles)	Guns/ mile
1916	Somme	452	14mls	32
1917	Ypres	575	3mls	192
1918	Arras	963	13mls	71
1918	Vimy Ridge	377	4mls	94

Activities

1. **Class discussion:** In what ways did the war become like the sieges of medieval times? (KU)
2. What do you understand by the strategy of attrition. (KU)
3. Describe the destructive power of the guns at Verdun using Sources 10.13, 10.14, 10.16 and the text. (KU)
4. How successful was Falkenhayn's policy of attrition at Verdun? Explain your answer. (KU)
5. Why could the big guns not provide a quick victory? (KU)
6. How useful is Source 10.13 as evidence about how soldiers felt about the war? (ENQ)

Source 10.16 This impression of the Verdun battlefield was painted by Georges Leroux and entitled 'Hell'.

11 Trench warfare

[F] Case study – The difficulties of attacking enemy trenches

The German defences

According to the Germans, nowhere on the entire Western Front did they have stronger defences than on the Somme. Here their trenches wound round the tops of gentle sloping hills giving them a clear view of the British positions. Since the chalky soil was easy to dig the Germans constructed an elaborate front line trench system. A mile or two behind these, on the next ridge, they dug a second line and then a third. In front of each were wide belts of wire whose barbs were sometimes two cm long. Ruined villages such as La Boiselle and Serre were turned into fortresses with machine-guns safely concealed among the rubble. Furthermore, the Germans had constructed redoubts on hillsides which gave them a particularly good firing position. While above ground these might appear simply as a criss-cross section of trenches, below ground they were like rabbit warrens. The Leipzig Redoubt for example, could accommodate 50 soldiers with beds, electric lighting, piped water and even a bakery!

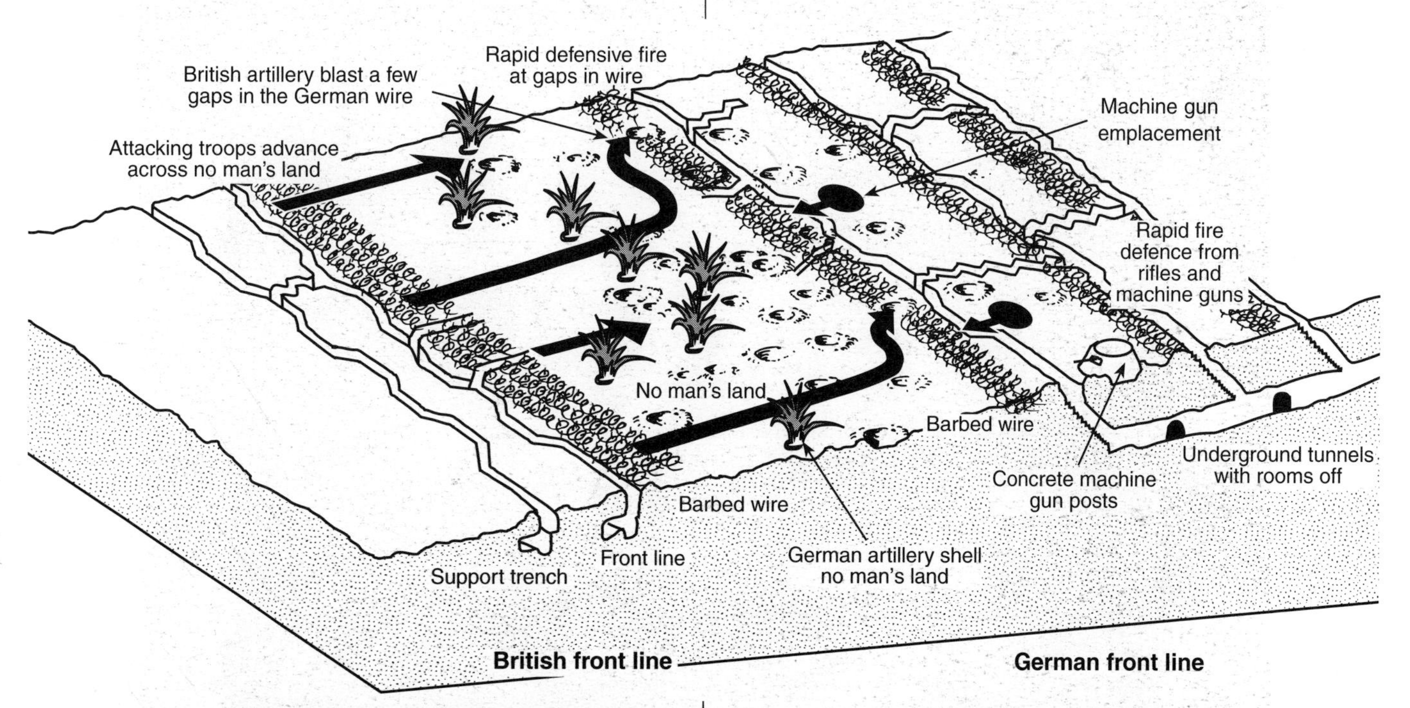

Source 11.1 A section of Somme front line showing the stretch of front line attacked by the 15th, 16th and 17th Highland Light Infantry.

Source 11.2 All along the Somme front the Germans created shell proof dug-outs sometimes 12m below ground.

The British preparations to attack

The Battle of the Somme was originally planned as a joint attack but Verdun meant that fewer French soldiers would be involved. Instead, centre stage would belong to the volunteers of Kitchener's army, an exciting prospect for the British public who talked openly of the coming 'big push'.

Meanwhile in France, the Germans watched the British army prepare for the attack. From their planes and observation balloons the Germans looked on with astonishment and joked about this army of Pals becoming 'cannon fodder' (sitting targets). They reckoned that their trench lines on the Somme could not be breached. Then on 24 June the British confirmed that they were not bluffing, when they began a week long bombardment to smash the German defences. It failed.

The attackers

On Saturday 1 July 1916, along a 14 mile long front, the volunteer army waited to go into battle. The experience of the Barnsley Pals was typical. Heavily laden with 30kg of kit and extra ammunition, they were to leave their trenches when the whistles blew and march uphill across ground where no one had walked in the open for two years. They were

Source 11.3 In a communication trench, British soldiers fix bayonets in preparation for the assault on 1 July 1916.

told that the bombardment had been successful and that crossing no man's land would be like walking in the park. Even so, as zero hour approached some anxiety was inevitable.

Source 11.4

> ***My feelings were very mixed as we waited to go over. ... We had no actual front line experience ... we'd no idea of trench fighting at all. That was the biggest disadvantage we had.***
>
> **Tommy Oughton, Barnsley Pals.**

Five miles down the line opposite the formidable Leipzig Redoubt, the men of the Glasgow 'Tramways', 'Boys Brigade' and 'Commercials' (15th, 16th and 17th Highland Light Infantry) adopted a different strategy. While British shells were still falling, they crawled to within 40m of the German wire. At 7.30 am when the bombardment ceased, they rushed the Leipzig Redoubt and were soon fighting hand to hand in the trenches and tunnels. However, when the attacks on either side failed, they were soon isolated. Furthermore, reinforcements could not get through the screen of German shells falling on no man's land and the Highland Light Infantry were driven out.

Meanwhile at Serre, the Barnsley Pals were in trouble ..

Source 11.5

> ***Our lads were going down in their waves, flop, flop, flop. They were walking across ... but even if we'd run across we'd still have been in the same fix because we couldn't have got through their wire. ... You couldn't get to the places where the machine guns were, they were in emplacements. Their wire was bundled in great rolls with just an odd gap between ... As soon as you made for that gap it was R-R-R-R-R. They had their guns on that gap.***
>
> **Frank Lindley, Barnsley Pals.**

It was a similar story all along the front. Opposite Sausage Redoubt most of the Hearts footballers of the 16th Royal Scots lay wounded in no man's land. Here, as elsewhere, the Germans had rushed from their deep dug-outs when the barrage lifted and poured bullets into the advancing British infantry while they were in the open. It is claimed that Kitchener's army of 'Pals' was destroyed within 10 minutes – hardly firing a shot in their own defence. Of the 60 000 men who attacked, 57 000 became casualties on what was the blackest day in British military history. It would take more than brave men and guns to capture a German trench.

Activities

1. Why were the German trenches on the Somme so strong? (KU)
2. How can you tell Tommy Oughton (Source 11.4) was a volunteer rather than a regular army soldier? (KU)
3. According to Frank Lindley (Source 11.5), why did the British attack fail? (KU)
4. Using Sources 11.1, 11.2 and the text find other reasons why the British Army found the German trenches on the Somme difficult to capture. (KU)
5. Why is Source 11.5 valuable evidence of the difficulties soldiers faced in attacking enemy trenches? (ENQ)

G/C NEW TECHNOLOGY (I) TANKS – AT THE SOMME AND CAMBRAI

Background

Despite firing two million shells from its 200 howitzers and 1500 guns, the British artillery had failed in its main task, to get the infantry across no man's land. The attacking waves of Kitchener's army had consequently failed to achieve a breakthrough, being mown down by German machine-guns 'like corn before the reaper'. General Haig however, was not too downcast at the failure of his human battering ram because he was about to launch a steel one!

The 'Landship'

Source 11.6 To the British they were 'Landships' or 'tanks' but when German soldiers first saw them they christened them 'Devil's coaches'.

Throughout 1915, work was progressing on a secret weapon which, it was hoped, would end the stalemate of trench warfare. For a while it was known as a 'Landship' since funding for it was provided by the navy when the army rejected the idea. The name of this weapon was subsequently changed to 'tank' due to its similarity to a water container and to conceal its real purpose.

In February 1916, Haig watched tanks being put to the test and immediately placed an order for them with the intention of using them on the first day of the Somme. However, he had not taken account of the time required to build them or to train their crews. It was not until August that the first 50 tanks arrived in France and Haig decided that they must take part in the third phase of the Battle of the Somme due to begin on 15 September 1916. This would go against the wishes of Lieutenant-Colonel Swinton, the 'father' of the tank who insisted that the tanks should be kept secret until a large number were available for one great attack. Winston Churchill, who as First Lord of the Admiralty, financed its development, had equally strong views on the matter.

Source 11.7

I was so shocked at the proposal to expose this tremendous secret to the enemy upon such a petty scale, and as a mere make-weight to what I was sure could only be an indecisive operation, that I sought an interview with the Prime Minister, Mr. Asquith.

Winston Churchill, 'The Great War'.

However, with casualties mounting and little progress being made, Haig took the decision to send the tanks into battle. Some say it was the right decision.

Source 11.8

... no general worth his salt would indefinitely postpone the use of a promising new weapon.

Andy Simpson, 'The Evolution of Victory'.

Into battle

By dawn on 15 September, 36 tanks were in position alongside Delville Wood. At 6.20 am the British artillery sent the Germans scurrying below ground while the tank engines roared into life. A German newspaper correspondent who witnessed the attack described what happened next ...

Source 11.9

We stared and stared as if we had lost the power of our limbs. The monsters approached slowly ... nothing could stop them ... Someone in the trenches said 'The devil is coming' ... Suddenly tongues of flame leapt out of the armoured sides ... shells whistled over our heads and the sound of machine gun fire filled the air. The mysterious creature had yielded its secret as the British infantry rolled up in waves behind the 'devil's coaches'.

Within four hours the British army had broken through two lines of enemy trenches and captured the fortified villages of Flers, Martinpuich and Courcelette and 4000 prisoners. The attack was an outstanding success. So much so that General Haig immediately placed an order for 1000 more tanks while the Germans frantically began to draw up plans for their own version.

The experience of fighting inside a tank

Source 11.10 A tank crew man wore a leather jacket and mesh visor to protect him from 'metal splash'.

Facing a tank may have been a terrifying experience for the Germans but being inside a tank was also pretty scary for the British crews.

Source 11.11

There is not one of us who will ever forget his first ride in a tank. We couldn't stand up, the engine roared, we couldn't hear, nor could we see. It was almost completely dark inside.

Sgt Littledale, Tank Corps.

Breathing was also difficult. There was little ventilation and as well as generating heat, the engine also produced carbon monoxide fumes. When its guns were firing, cordite fumes were also produced turning the air in the tank into a toxic cocktail which often made crew members pass out. It was even less comfortable being under fire as rifle or machine-gun bullets lead to 'metal splash', where the bullets' impact sent hot flakes of metal flying off the inside of the tank. Still this was preferable to the impact of an artillery shell which would simply blow the tank apart – crew and all!

Battle of Cambrai

Source 11.12 Tanks being brought up to Cambrai by rail. Each carried a fascine which could be dropped into a trench to act as a bridge.

As 1917 drew to a close, the tank had still not produced the breakthrough Haig had hoped for. However when plans were revealed for the Battle of Cambrai, it was clear that the mistakes of the past would not be repeated.

The terrain here was firm and the ground tanks ordered were more reliable and available in greater numbers. The town of Cambrai lay behind the Hindenburg Line, a specially constructed defensive system to which the German army had retreated in January 1917. Here the trenches were deep and wide and protected by 50m belts of barbed wire, pillboxes, and machine-gun posts. Nevertheless in more ways than one, the Germans were in for a surprise. On 20 November 1917, a ferocious five minute bombardment was the only warning they got before the tanks rumbled towards them.

Source 11.13

The German outposts ... were overrun in an instant. The triple belts of wire were crossed as if they had been beds of nettles and 350 pathways were sheared through them for the infantry. The defenders of the front trench scrambling out of the dug-outs and shelters to meet the crash and flame of the barrage saw the leading tanks almost upon them.

Captain DG Browne.

Another eye witness commented:

Source 11.14

The enemy appeared to be completely demoralised; prisoners were pouring in ... This was the first time that we had ever seen the artillery moving forward. It gave us all a great thrill; this attack of ours seemed to be developing into a great victory ... As far as we could see on the right they marched, three brigades in line, each battalion in fours. I cannot describe in words what a wonderful sight it was. The only thing missing was a band in front of each battalion. We cheered ... we were right through the Hindenburg Line and into open country.

Poor coordination between tanks and infantry and lack of reserves meant that the gains made at Cambrai were soon lost. However during the initial assault, the British had advanced more than ten kilometres into German territory over 'tank proof' trenches.

At Amiens in 1918, the tanks were even more successful. Six hundred British and French tanks, supported by aircraft but with no bombardment, stormed through the German lines, pushing the German army into general retreat. Cavalry at last broke out into the open countryside for the first time since 1914, but it was an iron horse that had made the breakthrough.

Activities

1. Describe a tank attack as seen by:
   a) a German soldier
   b) a British infantryman
   c) a tank crew member (KU)
2. Study Sources 11.7 and 11.8. With whom do you agree. Why? (ENQ)
3. Having studied all the Sources and the text, what conclusions would you make about the value of the tank in the First World War. (INV)

(II) GAS

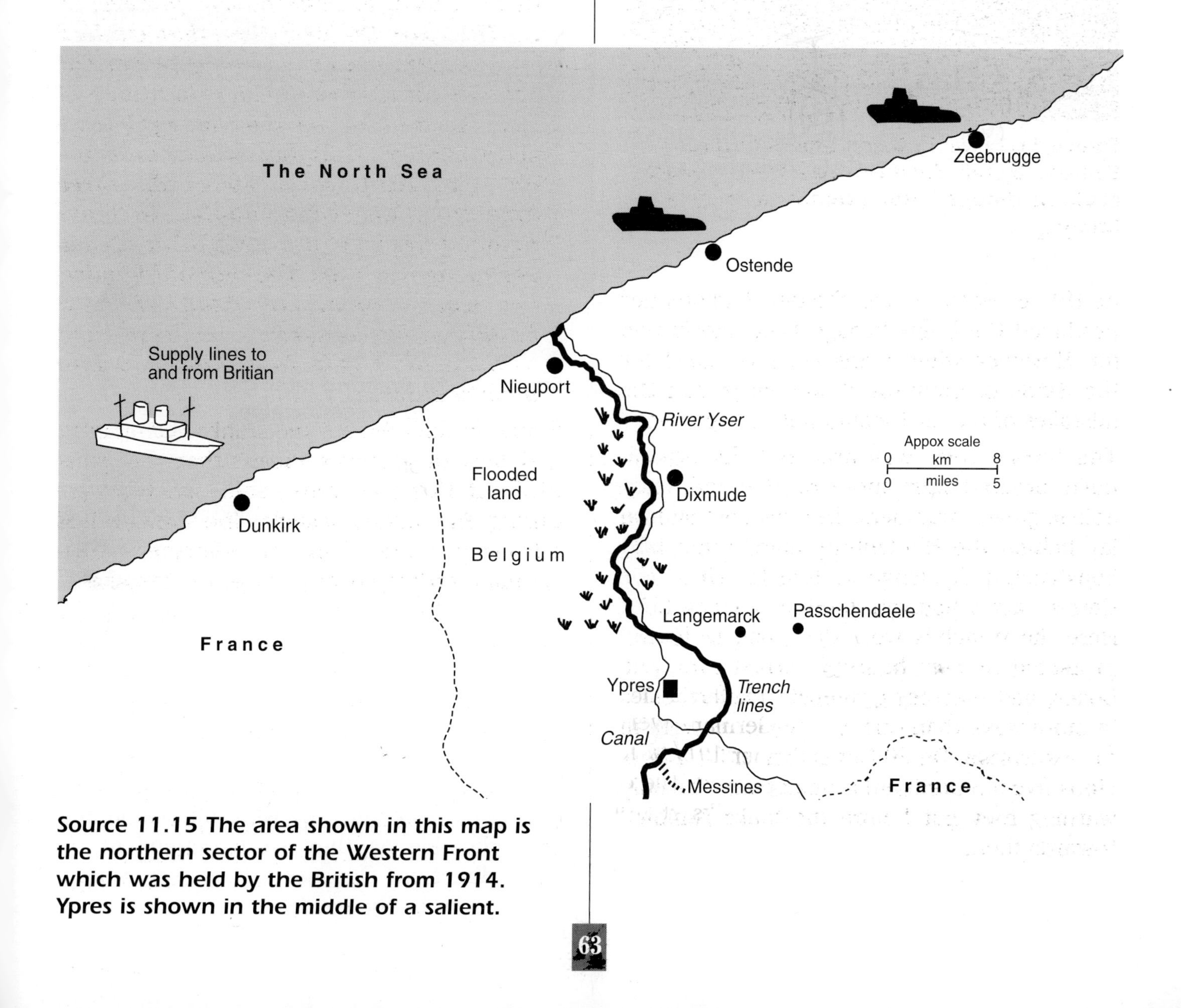

Source 11.15 The area shown in this map is the northern sector of the Western Front which was held by the British from 1914. Ypres is shown in the middle of a salient.

In 1914 the British had held on grimly to the Belgian town of Ypres. They could not afford to allow Dunkirk and the other French channel ports of Boulogne and Calais to fall into German hands (see Source 11.15 to discover why). The Germans were equally determined to hold on to the Belgian ports of Ostende and Zeebrugge because they were using them as bases for their U-boats (submarines) to attack British shipping. Ypres therefore was very important for both sides.

Ypres was surrounded on three sides by trenches. This is called a salient (see Source 11.15). In the spring of 1915 the Germans launched the first major attack of the year in the salient and used a new weapon – poison gas.

1915 – Gas

On the 22 April 1915 a member of the Queen Victoria Rifles witnessed the following scene in the trenches near Ypres.

Source 11.16

> ***We could see a low cloud of yellow-grey smoke or vapour. In the northerly breeze came a pungent and sickening smell that tickled the throat and made the eyes smart.***
>
> **Anthony Hossack, Queen Victoria Rifles.**

The Germans had released chlorine gas from canisters allowing it to blow in the breeze towards the allied trenches. The Algerian and French troops holding the line dropped their guns and fled in panic. Many of them did not stop running till they reached Ypres. Canadians who were in the line beside the attack took over the trenches vacated by the fleeing soldiers and held the line against the advancing Germans. The advantage was lost and counter measures were very quickly developed to counter future gas attacks.

Counter measures

The first gas masks were quite crude, as one soldier explained.

Source 11.17

> ***They consisted of a piece of muslin with a pad of cotton wool. In the event of a gas attack, we were told to urinate on the pad and bind it to our mouth and nose.***

These masks were of no use against any kind of poison gas and more sophisticated gas masks were developed to counter the effects of gas (see Source 11.18).

Source 11.18 Wearing later gas masks was very tiring and uncomfortable.

During the war, different gases were used – sometimes released from canisters and sometimes fired into enemy trenches in gas shells. The type of gas most feared by the troops was mustard gas since it had no colour or smell and burnt the skin, the eyes and the lungs. The normal gas mask was no defence against mustard gas which was so strong that it could remain for weeks in dug-outs and hollows in the ground to catch the unwary soldier. Gas attacks were used frequently by both sides during the war but they were unreliable and unpredictable as they were dependent on wind direction. One gas attack (see Source 11.19) went badly wrong:

Source 11.19

The gas was invisible and was carried by the wind towards the German trenches. However, the wind veered round and our fellows were gassed in consequence. They came past us with ghastly yellow faces from the effects of the gas and the buttons of their tunics had been changed to a green colour.

A Stuart Dolden, 'Cannon Fodder'.

Gas is estimated to have killed about 90 000 men and to have blinded or injured perhaps up to a million men, but it did not provide the generals with their breakthrough. It was as difficult to attack through gas as it was to defend, because wearing the gas-mask was very uncomfortable and exhausting as the soldiers were short of oxygen. Poison gas, although it caused large numbers of casualties, was not the technology to win the war.

Source 11:20 Soldier's song

Gassed last night and gassed the night before
Gonna get gassed tonight if we don't get gassed any more
When we're gassed we're sick as we can be
'Cos phosgene and mustard gas are much too much for me

They're over us, they're over us
One respirator for the four of us
Glory be to God that three of us can run
So one of us can use it all alone.

Activities

1. Explain the importance of the town of Ypres to Britain and Germany. (KU)
2. Write down the names of three different types of gas. (Try to find out more about their effects from your science teacher.) (KU)
3. Describe a gas attack using the text and Sources to help you. (KU)
4. Give two reasons why gas did not provide the generals with a breakthroughough. (KU)
5. What evidence is there that gas was used widely during the war. (KU).

(III) OF MINES AND MEN

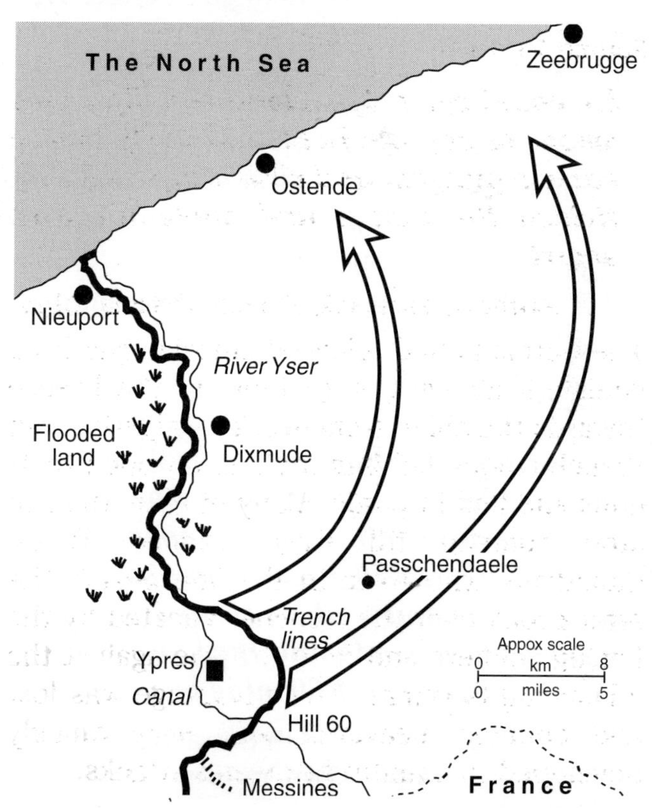

Source 11.21 The plan of 1917 – to break out of the salient and to capture the ports of Ostende and Zeebrugge.

The village of Passchendaele sits at the top of a ridge of gently sloping hills about six miles from Ypres. In 1917, after the costly failures on the Somme the year before, General Haig decided to launch a major new offensive from Ypres towards the Passchendaele and Messines Ridges. His objectives were to break out of the salient, capture the ports of Ostende and Zeebrugge and to drive the Germans out of their strong defensive positions in this sector.

Preparations – mines at Messines

To the south, Ypres was overlooked by the Messines Ridge which had been held by the Germans since 1914. From 1915 General Plumer had been working on a plan to knock the Germans off the ridge. He intended to dig 21 deep mine shafts below the German positions on the high ground, fill them with high explosive, and explode them all at once. This was slow work and the mines were not ready until June 1917. One of the mines had been dug at a German strongpoint called Hill 60. This mine was stuffed with the high explosive ammonal, ready to be set off at zero hour. At 3.10 a.m. on 7 June 1917 nervous British troops waited anxiously opposite the German positions at Hill 60. One in the front line wrote:

Source 11.22

It was an appalling moment. We all had the feeling 'It's not going'. And then a most remarkable thing happened. The ground on which I was lying started to go up and down like an earthquake. It lasted for seconds and then suddenly in front of us the Hill 60 mine went up.

Lt. J Todd of the 11th Battalion Prince of Wales Own Yorkshire Regiment.

The blowing of the mines along the Messines Ridge was a great success. All along the ridge the British troops captured the heights when the German defenders were blown sky high. However, the time taken in the planning and the digging of the mines, and the very localised nature of their effects meant that mines alone could not provide the break-through. General Haig was now poised to launch his attack from Ypres to try to break out of the salient. This was to be the next 'big push' to end the war.

The experience of a major battle

In July 1917 the British guns pounded the German positions in the salient around Ypres to herald the opening of a major battle. However, the major problem facing the British was that the Germans held all the high ground surounding the salient and were therefore able to see every move they made. This greatly helped the German gunners who were able to cause havoc amongst the advancing troops on 31 July.

Source 11.23

As we were struggling up to Minty's Farm one of the boys got hit with a huge shell fragment. It sliced him straight in two. He dropped his rifle and threw his hands up in the air, and the top part of his torso fell back on the ground. The unbelievable thing was that the legs and the kilt kept on running, just like a chicken with its head chopped off.

Lt. J Annan, 1st/9th Battalion Royal Scots.

Source 11.24 Holding the line in shell holes during the Battle of Passchendaele. The soldier manning the machine-gun in the foreground is Pte. Reg Le Brun. (See also Source 11.31.)

Despite the heavy barrage by the German guns the first waves of infantry achieved their initial targets comparatively easily. However, the soldiers soon realised that they were attacking a fortress as the Germans pulled back from their front lines to a well defended line of concrete bunkers and pill-boxes. From the safety of these structures the Germans defended ferociously and British casualties began to mount as all along the line the advance was held up. As one battalion moved towards what had been the village of Hooge it was pinned down – and the weather broke.

Source 11.25

We couldn't get the wounded away for there was nothing between us and the Germans. They were pasting us with shells and machine-gun fire and the rain kept pouring down. The trench began to fill up with water.

W Lockey, 1st Battalion Notts and Derbyshire Regiment.

The attack in August 1917 coincided with the wettest autumn on record in Belgium and the whole battlefield turned into a swamp. As the weather worsened the 'big push' got bogged down in the Flanders mud. The impossible conditions were described by an eye-witness.

Source 11.26

There was no chance of the infantry getting across. I watched them struggling like blazes through the frightful bog to get at the Germans. However, they were up to their knees in mud and by the time they got half-way across, it was virtually impossible for them to move either forward or back. Then the machine-guns started to pick them off.

Major Rory Mcleod of the Royal Field Artillery.

Passchendaele

The 'big push' of 1917 was known officially as the 3rd Battle of Ypres, but it was known to the soldiers as 'Passchendaele'. In August 1917 the British army slogged its way up the muddy slopes from the outskirts of Ypres but in September General Haig was advised by his field commanders that, in these conditions, a breakthrough was impossible and that the attack should be called off. Haig refused to listen and ordered that it should continue. He now believed that if a breakthrough was impossible, at least he could wear down the enemy by continuing the push on the German positions. As Falkenhayn had done in 1916 at Verdun, Haig decided to follow a policy of attrition. By September therefore, hopes of a breakthrough had gone and the plan to reach Ostende and Zeebrugge was abandoned. Instead, Haig decided to capture the village of Passchendaele on the high ground to give the British troops dry trenches for the winter. The slog through the mud was to continue.

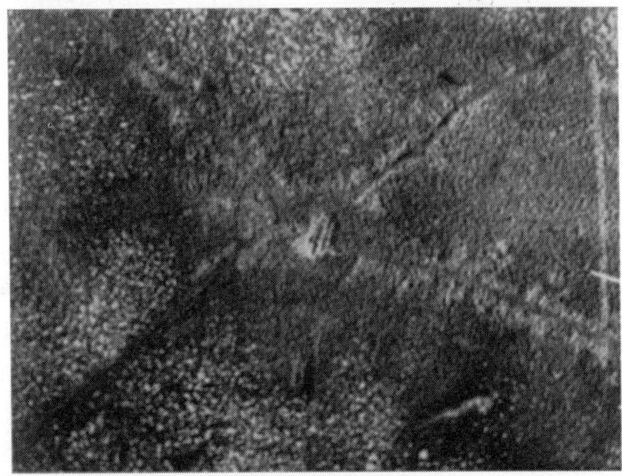

11.27 Passchendaele battlefield – the same area before and after the artillery bombardment.

The horrors of battle

The conditions experienced by the soldiers at Passchendaele in 1917 were dreadful. They were never dry, usually caked in thick mud – and the shelling and gunfire hardly ever let up.

Source 11.28

The whole area was utterly devastated, just a few bits of foundations left. There was no trace of the farms and barns that had been there in 1915, nothing but this ocean of mud and dumps and a few scattered pillboxes.

Gunner J Brown, Canadian Field Artillery.

Source 11.29

The salient was a dead loss. You had this Ypres-Yser Canal and you got the strangest feeling when you crossed it. You'd almost abandon hope. And as you got further out you got this awful smell of death. You could literally smell it. I wept when I came into the salient.

2nd Lieutenant HL Birks, Tank Corps.

Source 11.30

I came to hate that salient. It wore you down. The weather, the lack of rations, everything seemed to be against you. You were wet through for days on end. We never thought we would get out alive. You couldn't see the cloud with the silver lining. There wasn't one.

Lieutenant J Naylor, Royal Artillery.

Amidst the devastation were the horrific scenes of death and despair experienced by the soldiers.

Source 11.31

The shelling never let up. I heard someone calling for help. It was one of our infantrymen propped up on his elbow with his tunic open. I nearly vomited. His insides were spilling out of his stomach and he was holding himself trying to push all this awful stuff back in.

Pte. R Le Brun, Canadian Machine Gun Company.

Yet even in this carnage there was time for giving some of the dead a decent burial.

Source 11.32

> ***There was nothing at all except huge craters. They were full of water and the corpses were floating in them. Some with no heads. Some with no legs. We committed each one properly to his grave. The men all stood around and took their hats off for a moment, standing to attention. 'God rest his soul'. A dead soldier can't hurt you. That's how we looked at it. He was some poor mother's son and that was the end of it.***
>
> **Lieutenant P King, East Lancashire Regiment.**

It was not until 6 November 1917 that Canadian troops finally entered the ruins of Passchendaele. The five mile journey to Passchendaele through the lunar ladscape of mud and craters had taken 99 days and cost Britain and Germany each a quarter of a million casualties.

Activities

1. In what way did General Haig's objectives change between July and September 1917 at Ypres? (KU)
2. Put yourself in the position of a soldier fighting at Passchendaele. Write a letter to someone at home describing your experiences of war and their effects on you and your attitudes to the war. (KU)
3. What arguments could be put forward to suggest that the 3rd Battle of Ypres was a success for General Haig? (KU)
4. What is Lieutenant King's view of fighting on the front line? (ENQ)

12 TOTAL WAR

F/G WOMEN AT WAR

Women had wanted to be involved in the war from the start. Patriotic girls felt just as keenly about the war as their brothers or fathers in uniform.

Source 12.1

> ***I wanted to do my bit. My brother was at the Front and what was I doing? Serving at a table. What good was that?***
>
> **May MacDonald.**

In 1914 many young women worked in domestic service – that is, as housemaids, cleaners, cooks and nannies to the wealthy families in the country. For many it was an unpopular job with long hours and low wages, often as low as £2 per month for working from 6.00am until 9.00pm.

The war helped to bring about a big change in the lives of women. Half a million men volunteered for the army in 1914 and many jobs which had traditionally been done by men were gradually given over to women.

These included jobs working on the railways, on the buses and trams, in the police force, in coal mines as surface workers, as government employees in offices and even in the army and navy – though they could not fight, of course. In addition, the government needed workers to make munitions – shells and bullets for the war.

Source 12.2 Women at work at Gretna mixing 'devil's porridge', cordite for the shells.

Munitionettes

400 000 domestic servants left their jobs to find work making munitions and by the middle of 1917, more than three quarters of a million women were working in munitions factories. There they often worked 12 hour shifts making the shells and bullets necessary for the war effort.

To cope with the ever increasing demand for munitions, new factories and whole new towns were built such as Eastriggs and Gretna in Dumfriesshire. 11 000 women were employed in the munitions' factory at Gretna producing cordite for the shells and bullets. The work was always hard and dangerous, (in an explosion at Gretna in 1917 a munitionette was killed), but the work was well paid.

Source 12.3 One munitionettes's opinion of war work – 'Munition Wages'.

Earning high wages? Yus
Five quid a week
A woman, too, mind you,
I calls it dim sweet.

Afraid! Are ye kidding?
With money to spend!
Years back I wore tatters
Now – silk stockings, mi friend.

I've bracelets and jewellery,
Rings envied by my friends;
A sergeant to swank with,
And something to lend.

I drive out in taxis,
Do theatres in style.
And this is mi verdict –
It is jolly worth while.

Rosina Wyatt.

The biggest change for women came after 1916 when conscription was introduced and men were called up into the army in large numbers. The number of jobs for women now increased, and not only in munitions. Many became mechanics, window cleaners, bank clerks and a large number joined the 'Land Army' which was formed to replace the men who had left jobs on farms to join the army. On the farms they had to plough, sow and reap as the men had done before and the work was not easy.

Changing status

Many women now found a new freedom which came with increased wages and they began to do things which were unthinkable before the war such as going out unaccompanied, smoking in public places and going to cinemas and theatres with their female friends. In some occupations they even had to dress like men and to wear their hair short. Women gained self-confidence and eventually earned the grudging respect of many men for their efforts during the war.

"WE SHOULD MISS YOU, MARY, BUT YOUR UNDOUBTED TALENT SHOULD BE OFFERED TO THE NATION IF THERE IS A WOMAN'S BOMB-DROPPING CORPS."

Source 12.4 'Punch' cartoon, 18 August 1915.

At the end of the war many women gave up their jobs in favour of the men returning from the war. Some felt that this was only fair to the returning heroes. Other women held on to their jobs and new lives because the number of war casualties meant that there were many jobs which had no men returning to them.

In June 1918 women over the age of 30 were awarded the vote in recognition of the invaluable contribution made to the total war effort by women between 1914 and 1918.

Activities

1. In 1914, do you think women were regarded as equal to or inferior to men? Give one reason. (KU)
2. Why do you think domestic service was an unpopular job? (KU)
3. Look at Source 12.3. Why did this woman jump at the chance of working in a munitions factory? (KU)
4. Look at Source 12.4. What attitude does the man in the cartoon have about women working in wartime? How might he have changed this attitude by 1918? (ENQ)
5. How did the war affect and change the lives of women? (KU)

C CIVILIAN LIFE

The government felt that what was going on in Britain was almost as important as winning the war on the Western Front. Indeed they talked about Britain as the Home Front, suggesting that it was just as much part of the war as the battles in Europe.

Everyone in Britain was affected in some way by the war. Almost every family had a son or a father or a cousin in the war and many suffered the grief of losing a loved one in one of the many battles fought on the Western Front. To begin with there was a great deal of sympathy for those who lost a relative but as the war wore on and the casualty lists grew ever longer and almost every family was touched by grief, there was little room left for sympathy. Everyone was in the same boat.

The Defence of the Realm Act

The 1914–1918 war was the first war in which the full might of a country's resources like coal, iron, steel, textiles, chemicals and manpower had to be used to fight the war. In Britain the realisation that the country's resources had to be used brought about changes in industry, work on the land and in the everyday lives of the people.

On 8 August 1914 the government passed the Defence of the Realm Act (DORA). It gave the government powers to control what people did and meant that it could pass laws without asking parliament. There were many laws and regulations passed under DORA.

CENSORSHIP

It was thought important for the morale of people that they did not read the truth about military defeats and disasters. Newspapers were heavily censored, partly to stop the Germans getting vital information and partly to stop the people from getting depressed by bad news from the Front. As a result, newspapers twisted the truth, representing defeats as slight setbacks or even, as in the case of the cartoon in Source 12.6, as famous victories. One journalist commented:

Source12.5

> ***The Office of Censorship at first permitted us to mention that following a battle the dead on both sides were noticeable. A time came when it only allowed German dead on the battlefield. Later still no dead were permitted.***

From Lyn MacDonald, 'Voices and Images of the Great War'.

"SOMME" PUNCH.

Source 12.6 'News of the World' – 2 July 1916 – the day after the infantry attack in which 20 000 British soldiers died.

Many people saw the point of censorship, however. In the early months of the war worries about spies seemed more important than accurate newspaper reports, as this letter to *The Times* shows:

Source 12.7

> ***Sir, Is it not possible for the Press of England to take a stand against the spread of false information calculated to play the game of the Germans? The story of the annihilation of two well known regiments a few days ago and the meeting between Mr Churchill and Lord Kitchener today can only be of use to the Germans.***
>
> **'The Times', 28 August 1914.**

ALIEN REGISTRATION

Foreign citizens, even people who had lived and worked in Britain for years, were ordered to register as aliens. If they did not do so they could be liable for a substantial fine or even imprisonment.

DRUNKENNESS

When Irish labour arrived to build the Gretna munitions factory there was such concern in the Carlisle area about drunkenness and violence that the government passed laws controlling the hours of opening in public bars. The pubs could not stay open for as long and beer was watered down so that it was not as strong. It was against the law for a person to buy drinks for anyone else and people were taken to court for trying to buy girls a drink. In these ways throughout the country the government tried to reduce drunkenness and absenteeism from vital works. Drink was portrayed as 'the enemy's ally' to try to discourage over-indulgence.

INDUSTRY

The government decided to keep a very tight control over industry, hours of work, the amount and type of goods produced, wages earned and so on. However, in the first rush to volunteer, many men from key jobs like coalmining, steelworking, farming etc had joined the army, and it was soon realised that their jobs were crucial to the war effort so the government prohibited any more from joining up.

In addition, the government took on powers to order men to stop doing a particular job and to do one which was more useful to the war effort. This was known as Direction of Labour. Strikes were made illegal in certain industries (e.g. in munitions) and people complaining about their working conditions or pay were often branded as traitors. One worker in Glasgow during the war commented:

Source 12.8

> ***Longer hours, wage cuts, called a traitor if you tried to get your Union to help . . . I wondered if it was the Germans the Government was fighting or their own people.***
>
> **Erl Wilkie, shipyard worker.**

While Erl Wilkie complained that there were wage cuts in some cases, in others, the workers were compensated by higher wages than they had earned before.

CONSCRIPTION

In January 1916, the first law of its type ever in British history was passed, making it compulsory for fit men of a certain age to join the army. This was called the Military Service Act. It came about because the level of volunteers after 1915 could not keep pace with the frighteningly high level of casualties on the Western Front. People were understandably no longer as keen to enlist as they had been in 1914, as this extract shows:

Source 12.9

Excellent as the recruiting returns are, the need is vital and immediate for more men. There has been an overwhelming difficulty in making many eligible men understand that their services are vitally required.

'The Times', May 1916.

MILITARY SERVICE ACT
1916
EVERY UNMARRIED MAN
of
MILITARY AGE
Not excepted or exempted under this Act
CAN CHOOSE
ONE OF TWO COURSES:
(1) He can ENLIST AT ONCE and join the Colours without delay:
(2) He can ATTEST AT ONCE UNDER THE GROUP SYSTEM and be called up in due course with his Group.
If he does neither, a third course awaits him.
HE WILL BE DEEMED TO HAVE ENLISTED under the Military Services Act ON THURSDAY, MARCH 2ND 1916.
HE WILL BE PLACED IN THE RESERVE AND BE CALLED UP IN HIS CLASS.
as the Military Authorities may determine.

Source 12.10 The Military Service Act, January 1916.

Between 1914 and 1918 the government in Britain intervened in the lives of the British people more than at any time before as 'Total War' meant total involvement. In other ways the government was forced to take new measures – one of which was rationing of foodstuffs in response to the German U-Boat threat.

Actitivies

1. Look at the Sources and the text. Why was it necessary for the government to pass the Defence of the Realm Act? (KU)
2. Look at Sources 12.5, 12.6, 12.7 and the text. Why must you be careful when basing your views of events in the war on newspaper reports? (ENQ)
3. What are the arguments for and against censorship in wartime. (KU)
4. Look at all the Sources. Do you think DORA was a popular Act? Explain your opinion. (KU)
5. **Class discussion:** Was the government interference in people's lives during the war justified? (INV)

13 The razor and the noose

F/G The razor

In 1917 the German government took a desperate gamble to try to knock Britain out of the war. In a note to the Kaiser, the German naval chiefs thought that they could:

Source 13.1

> ***... wound England most seriously by injuring her trade. By means of the U-boat we should be able to inflict the greatest injury.***

Note from the German Navy to the Kaiser, 1917.

Source 13.2 A German submarine at work.

By 1917, Germany had 105 U-boats (submarines) and the Kaiser was assured by the Chief of the naval staff that he could force Britain to its knees before the summer harvest. He was also convinced that America would either not enter the war, or have no influence even if it did. This was to be a fatal mistake.

In February 1917 the Germans began their unrestricted submarine campaign which was to attack all shipping approaching or leaving Britain. The campaign was so successful that one ship in four was sunk by the U-boats.

Food supplies in Britain

Since 1914 the U-boats had been an increasing menace but in 1917, shortages in sugar, margarine, milk, tea, butter, bacon and pork – as well as in other foodstuffs – became critical. Some types of food were so scarce that people were prepared to fight for them.

Source 13.3

> ***At Wrexham a wagon laden with potatoes was surrounded by hundreds of people, chiefly women, who scrambled on to the vehicle. Several women fainted in the struggle and the police were sent for to restore order.***

'The Observer', 8 April 1917.

The danger to Britain was so great that the government was forced to act. In December 1916, David Lloyd George became Prime Minister and he took steps to maintain food supplies.

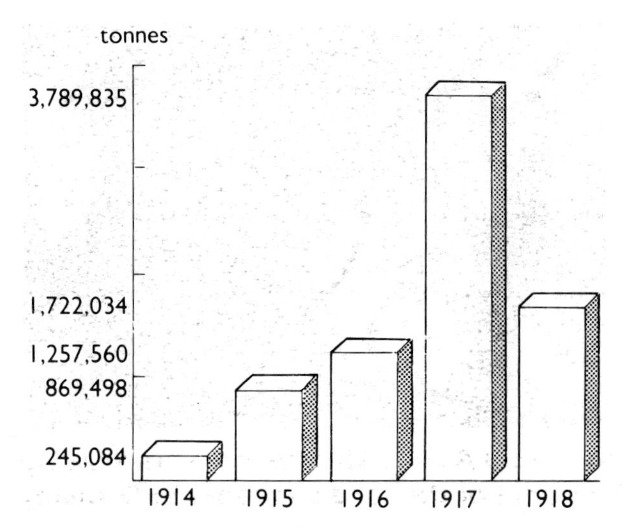

Source 13.4 The rising threat from U-boats. The chart shows the tonnage of British shipping lost in each year of the war.

Rationing

To begin with, people were asked to limit the amount of bread, meat and sugar which they ate each week, a voluntary rationing scheme.

RATIONED ITEMS	UNRATIONED ITEMS use with care	UNRATIONED ITEMS use freely no limit
SUGAR	TEA	EGGS
MEAT	MILK	POTATOES
BUTTER AND MARGARINE	JAM	FRUIT
BACON AND HAM	OATMEAL, RICE ETC.	FISH
	BREAD AND CHEESE	VEGETABLES
	BOTTLED FRUITS	

Source 13.5 Food was never in such short supply that Britons had to starve. However, some items were rationed as the table above shows.

However, as the shortages became worse in 1917, the government had to bring in a proper scheme of rationing to try to ensure that everyone got a fair share of certain basic foodstuffs – sugar, meat, butter, margarine, bacon and ham. Even so, the price of bread rose sharply and this affected the poor more than the rich.

Propaganda

The government began a poster campaign asking the British people to help beat the U-boats and to increase food supplies more land was planted. Public parks were often given over to potatoes, for instance and people were asked to grow more of their own food.

Source 13.6 The British people were asked to avoid waste in 1917 as one out of every four ships sailing out of British ports was being sunk by U-boats.

Convoys

Meanwhile, at sea, Lloyd George insisted that a convoy system should be adopted to protect British ships. Within weeks, it was shown to be a great success. Germany had just missed slashing Britain's jugular vein, but at the same time the Allied blockade was hurting Germany, like a noose slowly strangling the country.

Activities

1. What caused the food shortages in Britain in 1917? (KU)
2. What evidence is there that the U-boats were successful in 1917? (KU)
3. Identify five ways used by the British government to beat the threat of the U-boats. (KU)
4. Of what is Source 13.6 an example? (ENQ)
5. Find out about new forms of technology which were introduced to defeat the U-boats at sea. (INV)

C THE NOOSE

Before 1914 the French and British had agreed that Britain's Navy would immediately enforce a blockade of German ports on the outbreak of war to prevent supplies reaching Germany. As long as they believed that the war would be 'over by Christmas' the threat of a British blockade did not worry the Germans. The war, though, was not over by Christmas and by 1917, food and essential industrial raw materials were in short supply. To make matters worse, the harvest of 1916 failed and the winter of 1916–1917 became known as the 'turnip winter' as the German people were forced to eat animal fodder to survive. One girl remembered the problems.

Source 13.7

> ***Day after day we had to queue up for the barest necessities of life. My mother never ate her full rations but went without in order to feed Fritz and me a little better than our tiny share would have allowed her.***

Lilo Linke, 'The Great War, I was there'.

Source13.8 A soup kitchen in Berlin showing the extent of the food shortages in Germany.

Rationing was introduced in Germany in 1915 but by 1917, housewives found that supplies often ran out before they reached the head of the queue. To overcome the desperate shortages, the Germans began to produce substitute foods (*ersatz*), but these were often foul tasting and seldom healthy. For example, ersatz coffee was made from acorns. By 1917, each man was rationed to a quarter of a loaf per day and a tiny amount of butter. In that year, Germans ate only a quarter of the amount of meat which they had eaten in 1914. Millions of Germans were seriously underfed and an English woman married to a German and living in Berlin during the war said:

Source 13.9

> ***We are growing thinner every day ... we are gaunt and bony now. Our thoughts are taken up with wondering what our next meal will be.***

Weakness brought about by lack of nourishment during the war made the Germans more open to disease and when Spanish Flu struck Germany at the end of the war, perhaps as many as one million people died because they were unable to fight it.

Source 13.10 In Berlin, public parks were used for growing food since it was in such short supply.

The collapse of German morale

To make matters worse, the German gamble of unrestricted U-boat warfare had failed. Despite sinking over three million tons of British shipping in 1917, Britain was not defeated and the campaign had so annoyed the Americans that America entered the war in April 1917 on the side of the Allies. America was the world's strongest industrial power, had almost unlimited manpower, and could provide vast amounts of munitions and other raw materials necessary for fighting modern warfare. All this was now pitted against Germany.

Source 13.11 The arrival of the Americans and their industrial power spelt the end for German hopes of winning the war.

In Germany the strains of economic strangulation began to show in 1917 and the entry of America had a devastating effect on German morale. Unrest grew and strikes spread as many Germans came to see that their cause was now hopeless.

Source 13.12

The food situation is unbearable. The bread ration was reduced this spring. The potato supply has been insufficient. During the past month labourers had to live on dry bread and a little meat. Undernourishment is spreading. Conditions making for health are impaired. When we face this situation, we have to say 'our strength is almost spent'.

Friedrich Ebert, German politician, July 1917.

German industry also suffered shortages, especially of fuel and chemicals for munitions and by the end of 1917 the country's strength was almost at an end.

The final gamble

In October 1917, however, events in Russia gave the Germans hope for one last gamble. When revolution broke out in Russia, the Russians withdrew from the war. Germany could now concentrate all of its forces on the Western Front. General Ludendorff ordered that all available German forces were to be transferred there for one last major offensive before the Americans could arrive in large enough numbers to make a difference.

In March 1918 the German armies swept forward across the whole front and achieved the elusive breakthrough. In one day they recaptured all the ground taken during the Passchendaele offensive. In one week they recaptured all the ground lost at the Somme in 1916. In other parts of the front they broke through the French defences. Once more they advanced towards Paris and in March and April 1918 the Germans seemed to be close to victory – but the French and British armies were not destroyed. They retreated in good order and created a new defensive line. Troops were rushed to the Western Front from the Middle East and Italy to hold the line. In April the German advance faltered and the tide of battle swung back in favour of the British and French.

In one of the strange ironies of the war, the advancing German soldiers were dismayed to discover that the Allies could afford to abandon large quantities of brass, rubber, and copper as well as guns and shells. With American industrial might behind them they realised that the British and the French would never run out of essential supplies. General Fuller of the British Army said this of the German soldier:

Source 13.13

Wedged between his starving family and a hopeless future, his morale was shattered by the realisation that the succession of offensives since 21 March had been in vain.

The German soldiers now realised that they could not win the war. Even so, they fought on. In August a massed tank attack in which some 600 tanks took part, finally broke through their lines and pushed them back. The Germans retreated all along the line until the noose which had been slowly strangling Germany finally closed in November 1918 when they accepted the terms of an armistice and on the 11 November at 11 o'clock in the morning, the war to end all wars came to a silent conclusion.

Activities

1. Using evidence from the Sources describe the effects of the blockade on German civilians during the Great War. (KU)
2. Explain why Sources 13.7, 13.8, 13.9, 13.10 and 13.12 are valuable to a historian studying the effects of the war on Germany? (ENQ)
3. How important was a) the blockade and b) the entry of America in bringing about Germany's defeat in 1918? (KU)

14 Punishment of the Guilty

F/G President Wilson of America arrived in Europe in January 1919 as the leading figure at the Peace Conference. He came with a 14 Point Programme on which he hoped the peace would be based, but his ideas differed a lot from those of Lloyd George and Clemenceau (the French Prime Minister). Wilson wanted a peace in which Germany would not be punished. Clemenceau wanted to destroy Germany in order to protect France. Lloyd George did not want as harsh a peace settlement as Clemenceau, but he did want it to strengthen the British Empire. All three leaders had to take account of what their people wanted.

Public opinion

Public opinion in Britain and France was not yet ready to accept the kind of peace which Wilson suggested. Rudyard Kipling spoke for the ordinary people of both countries when he wrote:

Source 14.1

> ***These were our children who died for our lands: they were dear in our sight. We have only the memory left of their home – treasured sayings and laughter. The price of our loss shall be paid to our hands, not another's hereafter.***

Rudyard Kipling, 'The Honours of War'.

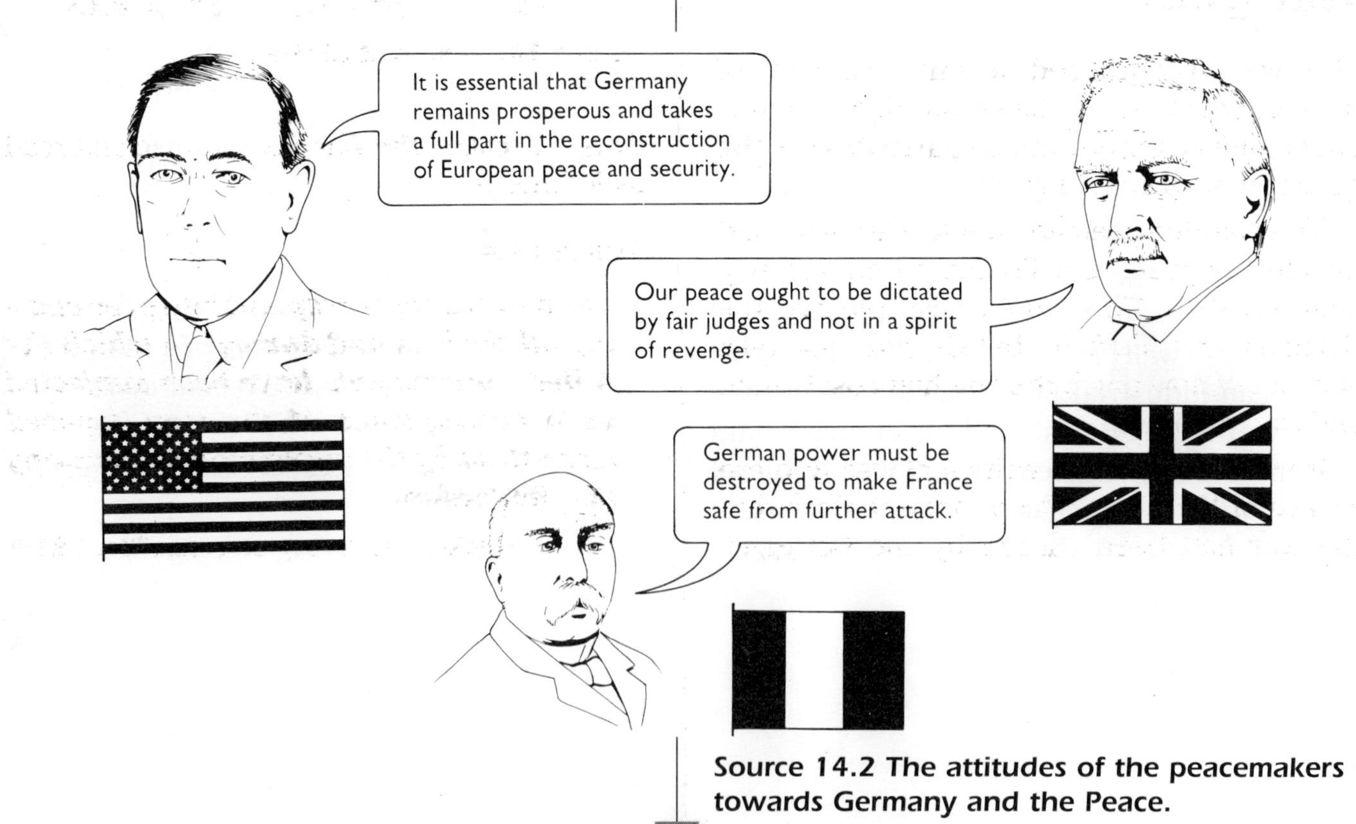

Source 14.2 The attitudes of the peacemakers towards Germany and the Peace.

The British and French had suffered too much: too many dead, wounded, maimed and disfigured soldiers; too much destruction on land and at sea. The time was not yet right for forgiving. 'The price of our loss shall be paid to our hands' – with these words Kipling said what many felt, that those who had been responsible for starting the war should be made to pay for it. In Britain and France the people believed that Germany had been responsible for starting the war and they demanded that the victory won by their armies at such a huge cost in men and materials should make their countries stronger and Germany weaker. There was a great desire to take revenge on the people whom they held responsible for the deaths of their loved ones.

THE COST OF THE WAR

War guilt

The war had caused a huge amount of damage which had to be repaired. As the war ended, the victor powers began to discuss the question 'who should pay?'

The solution seemed simple. Germany had invaded Belgium and France so should pay compensation. This would have pleased the Belgians and French, but it did not take account of how much the war had cost Britain and the Empire.

It was necessary to write a clause into the Treaty of Versailles which made it clear that the war had been caused by the Germans.

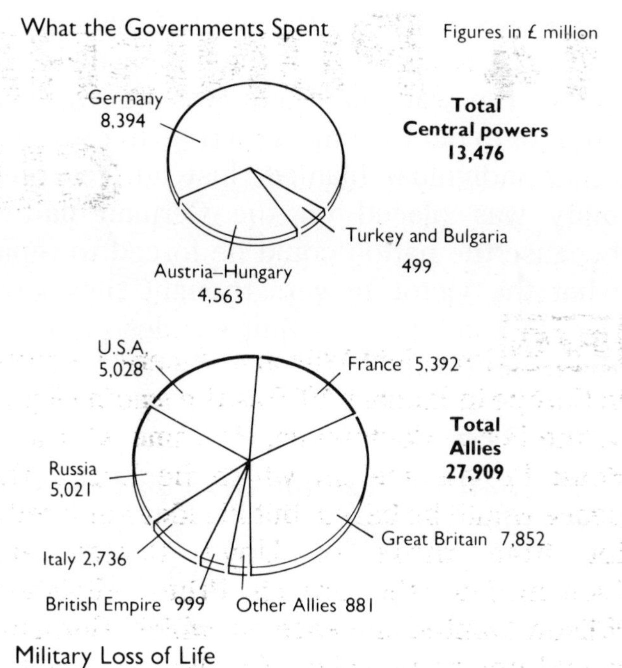

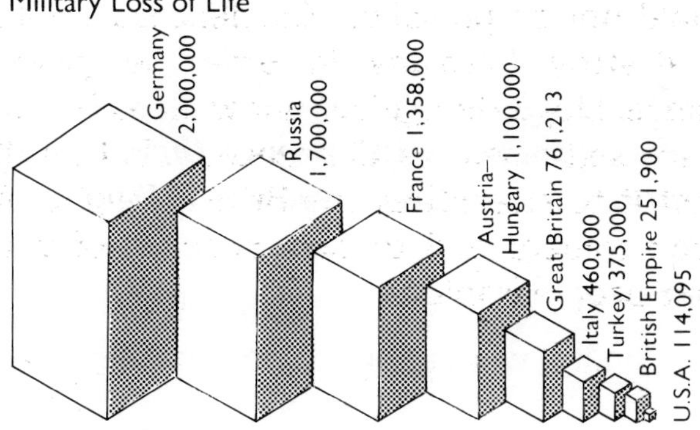

Source 14.3 The cost of the war.

This was called the War Guilt Clause and read as follows:

Source 14.4

> ***Germany accepts responsibility for causing all the loss and damage to which the Allied Governments have been subjected as a consequence of the war imposed upon them by the aggression of Germany and her allies.***
>
> **Article 231, Treaty of Versailles, 1919.**

There was no doubt that certain individuals had been responsible for actions which had led to the war, but there was no vigorous attempt to put the Kaiser on trial, nor was any other individual blamed. Instead, responsibility was placed on the German nation, because the nation could be forced to repay what the victor powers thought they were due. In London, Sir Arthur Geddes promised the people that:

Source 14.5

We shall squeeze the German lemon till the pips squeak.

Sir Arthur Geddes.

Even Lloyd George was eventually heard to remark:

Source 14.6

The Germans must pay to their last farthing and we shall search their pockets for it.

David Lloyd George.

The 'guilty' were about to be punished!

Activities

1. What word best describes the type of peace wanted by a) Clemenceau and b) Wilson? (KU)
2. Why were Clemenceau's ideas more acceptable to ordinary people? (Use Sources 14.2 and 14.3) (KU)
3. Why was Germany to be punished? (KU)
4. **Class Discussion**: Was it fair to blame the German nation for having caused the war? (Refer to Chapter 7). (INV)

C THE TREATY OF VERSAILLES

Clemenceau's victory

At the Peace Talks, Wilson and Lloyd George had urged moderation as they did not wish to leave Germany with a desire for revenge. However, between January and May 1919, the tide swung against them and in favour of Clemenceau.

Wilson's decline

The change in leadership at the Conference happened for three main reasons. Firstly, an attempted assassination of Clemenceau gained the old Prime Minister a great deal of sympathy.

Secondly, Wilson's views of American involvement in world affairs were not shared by all of his fellow countrymen. At home his party lost control of the Senate and from then onwards he no longer spoke for all America. The American Congress eventually refused to sign the treaty thus isolating America from Europe and from the new League of Nations.

Thirdly, public opinion in 1919 would not have accepted a peace which was not seen to curb German power. When the German delegation was ordered to the Hall of Mirrors in the Palace of Versailles therefore, they were presented with a dictated peace which reflected the views of Clemenceau much more than had been originally expected (refer back to Source 2.10).

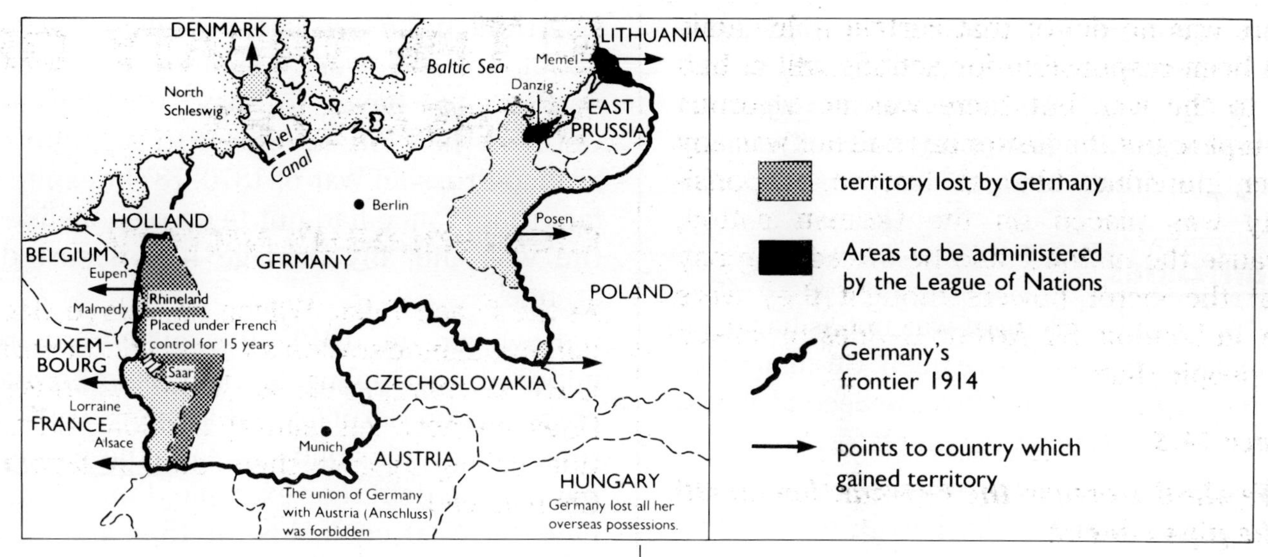

Source 14.7 German territorial losses at Versailles.

The terms of the Treaty of Versailles

On 7 May 1919 the terms of the Peace were presented to the Germans. The headline below appeared in the *Daily Record* on 8 May 1919.

Source 14.8

> ***Peace Treaty for Germany stern but just.***
> ***The Allies' Terms***
> ***French frontier of 1870 restored***
> ***£5,000,000,000 indemnity***
> ***Allied troops on Rhine for fifteen years***

The Germans who were presented with the terms were shocked. Inside Germany a myth was already developing that the German army had not been defeated in the field and that therefore the Germans should have been treated as equals at the peace conference. This arose because the allies did not invade Germany but instead accepted the surrender while the German army was still in France and Belgium. However, the terms were a clear statement that Germany was a defeated nation, but while they might have felt anger at the terms, there was nothing which they could do as the army was not in a position to re-open hostilities.

The Treaty of Versailles contained over two hundred clauses but the most important sections dealt with war guilt, reparations, territorial adjustments and German disarmament.

WAR GUILT

In Article 235 of the treaty, Germany and its allies had to accept responsibility for causing the war (see Source 14.4). However, the German delegation at Versailles made the following statement which was also reported on the *Daily Record*'s front page in Scotland on 8 May 1919.

Source 14.9 The German Reply: Spirited repudiation of Blood-Guiltiness.

> ***It is demanded of us that we shall confess ourselves to be the only ones guilty of the war. Such a confession in my mouth would be a lie. The German Government's action and omissions in the tragic twelve days of July certainly contributed to the disaster, but we energetically deny that Germany and its people, who were convinced that they were making a war of defence, were alone guilty.***

Count Brockdorff-Rantzau, 'Daily Record', 8 May 1919.

The German denials were not heeded, however and they were ordered to sign the treaty. On 28 June 1919, five years to the day since the fateful shootings in Sarajevo, the Germans signed the Treaty of Versailles.

TERRITORIES

The territorial settlement was not as harsh on Germany as it might have been. Germany was not divided (as it was after the Second World War), nor did it lose very much territory.

Alsace and Lorraine, which Germany had taken from France in 1871 were returned to France immediately. Parts of Germany were given to Belgium and Denmark. To the east of Germany, a new country was formed, Poland. The former German city of Danzig was to be a free city under the control of the League of Nations but with access to Poland. This had the effect of dividing Germany in two (see Source 14.7) with East Prussia being separated from the rest of Germany by a corridor of land stretching to Danzig. Germany also lost to Poland the coalfields of Silesia.

In addition, Germany also lost all of its overseas possessions, with the majority going to France and Britain. However, Germany remained a large and important country in the centre of Europe.

REPARATIONS

The 'War Guilt Clause' was included to allow the allies to force the Germans to pay reparations, to help meet the cost of repairing the damage caused by the war. The figure set was £5 000 000 000 – of which £1 000 000 000 was to be paid within two years, despite Germany's desperate economic condition in the aftermath of war.

Although the Germans complained bitterly about this, it was common for defeated nations to have to pay compensation. Germany had forced France to pay after the Franco-Prussian War of 1870–1871 despite the fact that France had not been responsible for the war and any damage had occurred in France!

However, in 1919, the allies not only imposed a crippling amount of reparations payments on Germany but in many ways they took away their ability to earn the money to pay off the debt. For example, France was to have the Saar coalfields for 15 years, Poland was given the Silesian coalfields, and Germany was stripped of the few overseas possessions it had. If Germany could not earn how could it be expected to pay?

MILITARY

The allies believed that the main causes of the war had been the arms race and German militarism. After the war they were determined to destroy German military power. The German army in the future was not to exceed 100 000 men and Germany was not permitted to have a navy beyond a handful of surface vessels. They were to have no U-boats and were not allowed an air force. The German Fleet was to be handed over to the British in 1919 at Scapa Flow. However, in one last act of defiance, the German commanders ordered the scuttling of the whole fleet – that is, it was sunk deliberately – and so Britain was denied the prize of the German navy. In addition, the border between France and Germany, the Rhineland, was to be occupied by allied forces for 15 years and Germany was not permitted to station any troops in that whole area.

To the Germans these terms were humiliating. For a country the size of Germany, an army of 100 000 was not enough to defend its borders from any attack and Germany was left totally defenceless. Having an army of occupation in the Rhineland was also deeply embarassing to a once proud nation.

In the Hall of Mirrors where in 1871 the German Empire had been founded after the Franco-Prussian War, the new German government was forced to accept the Treaty of Versailles as a dictated Peace. The Allies believed that they had framed a treaty which was 'stern but just', but the reaction from within Germany was one of shock. The whole German nation was blamed for the outbreak of war in 1914 and German public opinion was outraged at the humiliation of Versailles and that day the *Deutsche Zeitung* printed as its leading story this call to the German nation.

Source 14.10 Vengeance! German Nation!

Today in the Hall of Mirrors a disgraceful Treaty is being signed. Never forget it! On the spot where, in the glorious year of 1871, the German Empire in all its glory began, today German honour is dragged to the grave. Never forget it! The German people, with unceasing labour, will push forward to reconquer that place among the nations of the world to which they are entitled. There will be a vengeance for the shame of 1919.

Deutsche Zeitung, 28 June 1918.

Those non–Germans who also privately believed that Germany had been treated too harshly and that such a Peace would not last, believed that changes to the Treaty might be possible through the workings of the newly formed League of Nations.

Activities

1 Why did Wilson, Clemenceau and Lloyd George have such different views on how Germany should be dealt with after the war. (KU)

2 Describe the changing roles of Wilson and Clemenceau at the Peace Conference of 1919. (KU)

3 Explain the importance of Wilson losing control of the Conference? (KU)

4 How did the Germans react to the accusation of War Guilt? (Source 14.9) (KU)

5 Compare the 'Daily Record' (Source 14.8) and the 'Deutsche Zeitung'. (Source 14.10).
a) 'Stern but just'. To what extent does the German paper agree with this statement? (ENQ)
b) Why should historians studying Versailles be cautious when using sources like these? (ENQ)

6 **Class exercise**: Divide the class in two. One half should write essay a) while the other half should write essay b). Follow up with a class discussion in which both sides of the argument are identified and a conclusion arrived at. (KU)
a) Write an essay defending the Treaty of Versailles as 'just'.
b) Write an essay attacking the Treaty of Versailles as 'unjust'.

15 THE LEAGUE OF NATIONS

F/G

RECONSTRUCTION: A NEW YEAR'S TASK

Source 15.1 Rebuilding the world – the view of 'Punch', 1919.

There had been many wars in the history of the world but none had the impact in suffering of the Great War. The enthusiasm which had greeted the coming of war in 1914 had been replaced by the hope that the Great War would be the war to end all wars.

The American President, Woodrow Wilson, seemed to be in tune with the popular mood when he said:

Source 15.2

Many terrible things have come out of this war ... but some beautiful things have come out of it. Wrong has been defeated ... people that were suspicious of each other can now live as friends ... in a single family. Distrust is cleared away. We are brothers and have a common goal.

Wilson looked back to the years before 1914 and believed that the causes of the war were to be found in the arms race which had led to countries feeling insecure. In turn countries had formed alliances which had increasingly challenged opponents until a spark in 1914 had set off the war. Wilson believed that an international organisation was needed which would allow nations to talk openly to each other to prevent the kinds of mistakes made before 1914 which had led to war. He called this organisation the League of Nations.

President Wilson thought that the League should keep the peace and bring about international disarmament. In joining, every member covenanted (promised) that it would support the League and the League had the power to ask for the support of all member nations in an emergency.

Source 15.3

Should any country resort to war ... it shall be the duty of the council ... to recommend what force shall be used to protect the Covenant of the League.

Article 16, League Covenant.

President Wilson hoped that all the major European powers would be members and that America would play a leading role in the

League's work. He also wanted the League to take an interest in other aspects of world affairs and to help rid the world of some long-lasting problems like slavery, ill-health and poor housing.

The organisation of the League

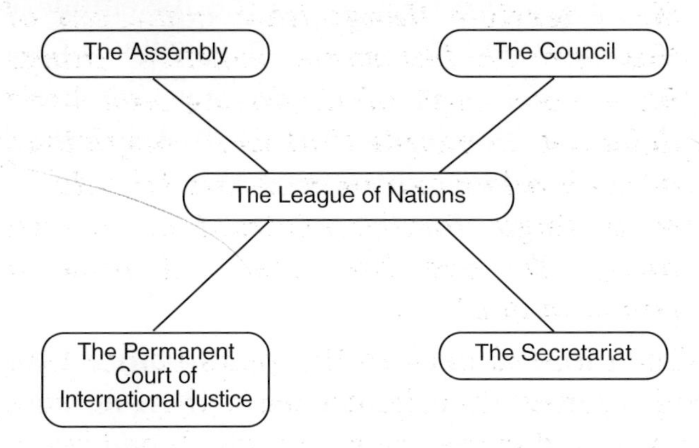

Source 15.4

Every member country had the right to send representatives to the **Assembly** of the League, a body which would discuss any problems and try to agree on solutions hopefully without the need for war. The most powerful countries in the League were to be allowed on the **Council** which took the final decisions about world peace-keeping. This consisted of only eight countries including Britain and France. The **Secretariat** provided secretaries, translators, investigators and experts to help the League do its work. The **International Court of Justice** acted as judge in the case of any international dispute on such things as boundaries.

Immediate problems for the League

To begin with there was great enthusiasm from many people for the League and rallies and demonstrations in support of the League were held. However, from the very beginning the League was faced with difficulties.

In 1919 America seemed destined to lead the League and to make it a truly worldwide organisation. The American Senate, though, thought otherwise and did not want America to be involved in the disputes of other nations. They rejected the Treaty of Versailles, Woodrow Wilson was defeated in a presidential election and America did not join the League.

THE GAP IN THE BRIDGE.

Source 15.5 America fails to bridge the gap. It did not provide the keystone for the bridge.

15.6 A League of Nations rally 1921.

As well as America not joining, neither Russia nor Germany were allowed to join. Germany because France would not allow it and Russia because it had gone through a revolution and was now a communist country. Russia was not trusted by Britain and France.

As a result, the League of Nations' two main members were Britain and France and it looked suspiciously like a club whose main aim was to ensure that the terms of the Treaty of Versailles would be maintained and to keep Germany under the control of France. This was not a good start for the League.

Other weaknesses

The decisions taken by the Council or the Assembly normally had to be unanimous – agreed by everyone. This was very difficult to achieve in crisis situations and if any country did not vote with the League, the League could not take action.

The League of Nations had no army of its own so it could not force countries to accept its decisions. Instead it would simply rely on the voluntary cooperation of its members and this was not always guaranteed either. With no standing army the League was regarded by the French, for example, as 'toothless'. If a country decided to go to war, how was the League supposed to take effective action against it if it had no forces at its disposal? To the French this was a major drawback from the very beginning.

OVERWEIGHTED

PRESIDENT WILSON: "Here's your olive branch. Now get busy."
DOVE OF PEACE: "Of course, I want to please everybody, but isn't this a bit thick?"

Source 15.7 'Punch' magazine suggested in 1919 that the job of peace-keeping might be a bit much for the League of Nations.

Keeping the Peace

In 1921 when the League began its work there was certainly plenty of optimism around for the League to succeed and in the early 1920s the League's prestige grew. When disputes arose they were brought to the Assembly of the League and debated. When called upon, the Council of the League took decisions backed by the League as a whole and settled various disputes. Jan Smuts of South Africa was one of the optimists:

Source 15.8

Mankind is once more on the move. The League may well be destined to mark a new era in the Government of Man and become a guarantee of peace. I am confident that the League will prove the path of escape for Europe out of the ruin brought by this war.

Jan Smuts, South African President.

In 1921 Sweden and Finland were involved in a dispute over the ownership of the Aaland Islands. The League intervened and arranged a settlement which both countries accepted. Further dispute was avoided. In the same year it managed to persuade Serbia to remove its troops from Albania by threatening to impose economic sanctions (which meant that no member country would trade with Serbia). Remembering that the Great War had begun from a small dispute involving Serbia, the League's success was all the more welcome. In 1923 the League settled a major dispute between Italy and Greece which threatened to erupt into war and two years later the League settled a further dispute in the Balkans between Greece and Bulgaria.

By 1925 therefore the League had been involved in the settlement of several potentially dangerous disputes between nations and peace had been preserved. In 1926 the

League of Nations finally accepted Germany in as a full member, not only to the Assembly but also on to the Council. A new era of cooperation between former enemies seemed to have dawned.

The League had provided a meeting place where international problems could be discussed and resolved through negotiation. At the League, representatives from different countries had met and become friends which was an important way of building up trust between nations. By 1926 the world seemed to be poised on the brink of a new system of international order.

Activities

1. Why was the League of Nations set up after the First World War? (KU)
2. How was the League of Nations organised? Look at Source 15.4 to help you anwer. (KU)
3. What benefits did President Wilson believe would come from having a League of Nations? (KU)
4. What were its two main aims? (KU)
5. What handicaps did the League have from the very beginning? (KU) (Write about non-members, links with Versailles and other weaknesses)
6. How did the League try to keep the peace in the 1920s? (KU)

C DISARMAMENT AND SECURITY

Disarmament had always been one of the main parts of President Wilson's plan for the new post-war world. It had been one of his 14 points:

Source 15.9

National armaments shall be reduced to the lowest point consistent with national safety.

Woodrow Wilson, Address to Congress, January 1918.

At Versailles, however, the French had insisted that Germany should be completely disarmed because they feared the power of a Germany determined to get revenge. In addition, the French were not happy with the League of Nations as they believed it to be ineffective without any kind of army to control international behaviour. When America withdrew from European affairs after the Senate rejected the Treaty of Versailles, the French became even more concerned that they might be left to face Germany alone in the future. As a result the French were opposed to reducing the level of their armaments and would not readily enter discussions about disarming without being given specific guarantees about their security from a future possible German attack. Clemenceau said in 1919:

Source 15.10

I am not a pacifist ... I wage war. In foreign policy I wage war. Always, everywhere, I wage war ... and I shall continue to wage war till the last quarter hour.

Georges Clemenceau.

French security

The fear of a future attack by Germany and the concerns about the League of Nations' weaknesses spurred the French into building a system of alliances against Germany. By 1927 these alliances had encircled Germany.

Source 15.11 French alliances 1920–1927.

1920 – Belgium
1921 – Poland
1924 – Czechoslovakia
1926 – Romania
1927 – Yugoslavia.

Source 15.12 The French Alliances 1920–1927.

German security

In 1923 the French exposed the German weakness when they invaded the area of the Ruhr to take German coal because Germany was not keeping up with the reparations' payments demanded by Versailles. The Germans were humiliated but, being totally disarmed, were unable to prevent the French occupation.

German security was further threatened by the new powers on its eastern borders, Poland and Czechoslovakia, both of which retained large armies and levels of armaments and when they both signed alliances with France by 1924, the German fear of invasion strengthened.

In the following year the leading German politician, Gustav Stresemann, began a policy which he hoped might lead to a softening of the Treaty of Versailles in Germany's favour and to a reduction in the threat to Germany's borders. He reached agreements with France and Britain hoping to create the conditions in which France might be prepared to begin disarming. At the same time, however, Germany also signed a secret treaty, the Treaty of Rapallo 1922, with Russia and was secretly rearming by building aircraft and tanks in Russia.

Steps towards disarmament

In 1924 the French and Germans re-negotiated a deal on reparations' payments which took the heat out of the occupation of the Ruhr and led to improved relations between France and Germany. Stresemann tried to reassure the French that Germany intended to be a good neighbour although he did want to make Germany the equal of France again.

Source 15.13

Stresemann was an intense nationalist but he saw that Germany's interests might be better served by diplomacy rather than showing one's teeth.

Wiskemann, 'Europe of the Dictators'.

In 1925 Germany signed a series of agreements with the French called the Locarno Pact by which they agreed that their common border was now fixed for all time and that neither side would go to war again to try to alter the border. In the following year, 1926, Germany was admitted to the League of Nations and was given a permanent seat on the Council. In 1928 by the Kellogg–Briand Pact, many countries, including France and Germany, said that they would no longer use war as an instrument of their national policy.

With relations between France and Germany now as good as they had been for many years, the time seemed right to begin serious talks on general disarmament and a Preparatory Commission was set up to prepare the ground for a full scale disarmament conference to take place.

Source 15.14 Gustav Stresemann.

Source 15.15 Ten years on – and by 1929 very little progress on disarmament had been made.

The Disarmament Conference

It took the Preparatory Commission three years to organise the conference which, it was hoped, would bring about a significant reduction in the arms of the world's major powers and make the world a safer place. However, by the time the conference met, conditions in the world had changed amidst a rising tide of aggression and a serious economic depression in Europe.

JAPAN

In 1931, using the pretext of a small disturbance on a Japanese controlled railway line, the Japanese invaded Manchuria which was part of China. The League sent investigators to find out who was to blame for the trouble. This group took two years to publish its report and by this time, Manchuria was under Japanese control. When Japan ignored the League, no action was taken. The League failed its biggest test as a peace-keeper.

Source 15.16 Japan makes a doormat of the League.

ITALY

The Italian leader, Benito Mussolini had striven to improve the Italian economy and the armed strength of Italy to the point where he could claim to challenge Britain and France's dominance of the Mediterranean and North Africa. He did not feel himself bound by international agreements and often said so:

Source 15.17

> ***Words are a very fine thing: but rifles, machine-guns, warships, aeroplanes and cannons are still finer things – right unaccompanied by might is an empty word.***

Benito Mussolini, 1929.

THE ECONOMIC DEPRESSION

In 1929 there was a huge crash in the American stock markets and as Europe was dependent on American money, every European economy was hit. Industries went out of business, savings were wiped out overnight and inflation and unemployment soared. Countries like Britain and France became more concerned with their own economic problems than with international events. Meanwhile Germany was hit particulary badly by the effects of the depression.

GERMANY

Ever since 1919, many people in Germany desired nothing more than to have revenge on France for the humiliation of Versailles. While times were good and people were in jobs and earning money, these feelings simmered below the surface. In the years 1929–1932, Germany suffered mass unemployment with as many as six million Germans out of work. In these conditions it was easier for the feelings of hatred and bitterness to surface again and for all Germany's troubles to be blamed on Versailles and the French. The Nazis, an extreme nationalist party led by Adolf Hitler, became more popular after 1929 and in 1933 he became Chancellor of Germany. His views on disarmament and security were clear:

Source 15.18

We demand the abolition of the Treaty of Versailles ... We demand land and territory for the nourishment of our people ... We demand equality in armaments.

Programme of the Nazi Party.

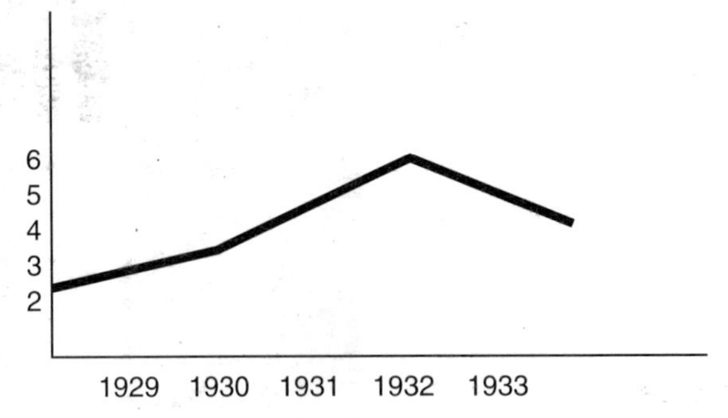

Source 15.19

Unemployed in milions in Germany 1929 to 1932. This rise coincided with the rise of the Nazi Party's fortunes.

Programme of the Nazi Party.

The collapse of disarmament

In these changed international circumstances the negotiations on disarmament collapsed. Hitler walked out of the conference in protest at the French position on German arms. Although the conference continued into 1934, no one was under any illusions that any of the major powers were likely to consider disarming seriously as the international situation deteriorated.

Activities

1. How did French concerns about their security affect their attitude towards disarmament? (KU)
2. In what ways did the policies followed by Stresemann in Germany help to bring disarmament closer? (KU)
3. Describe in detail why, by 1933, disarmament talks were doomed to failure. (KU)
4. What is the view on disarmament in Source 15.16? (ENQ)
5. **Class discussion:** Why was progress on disarmament so slow during the 1920s? (KU)